Carousel

Stories and Poems

By Hainault Creative Writers
© Hainault Creative Writers

ISBN 978-0-9552894-1-5

Published by Hainault Writers 2009

Hainault Writers
Hainault Forest Community Centre
100b Manford Way
Chigwell
Essex
IG7 4DF

Reg. Charity 308119

Printed and bound in Great Britain by
Trade Print Europe
72 New Bond Street
London W1S 1RR
www.printeurope.co.uk

CONTENTS

Adult Learners' Week
Awards

THIS IS TO CERTIFY THAT

Hainault Writers Group

WERE

Nominated

FOR A

Group Learners'
Award

in recognition of their achievement
in learning together as a group and
of the contribution this has made
to the community

Alan Tuckett

Alan Tuckett
Director, The National Organisation for Adult Learning

Margaret Davey

Margaret Davey
Chair, National Advisory Committee

NIACE
THE NATIONAL ORGANISATION
FOR ADULT LEARNING

SPONSORED BY

WRITTEN WORD

SPOKEN WORDS FROM LIPS ARE HEARD THEN LOST
UPON THE BREEZE
WRITTEN WORDS BY HAND WHEN READ REMAIN
FOR AN ETERNITY

Hainault Creative Writers Group

Acknowledgments

Mick Willis MBE
and the Staff
at Hainault Community Centre
for their help and support. Jill, Jean,
Dave, Frank and Cliff

Alan and Kathleen Hemmings for their assistance in getting the manuscript ready for printing.

Ivy Brown, our Member who designed and painted the front and back cover of the book.

Carousel. A Merry Go Round for easy riders.
Also a slide turntable for projecting pictures on a screen.
Carousel our book, is a projection of words
From a Writers mind onto a blank white page
That can give as much pleasure to a reader
As a rider on a Carousel.
With its many Stories and Poems
One can get on or off at any page
And the book is an admirable companion
For a journey by Bus or Underground

At a price comparable with many Magazines.

FOREWORD

Following the gratifying success of our last book
'Memories of Hainault', 'CAROUSEL'
is our seventh publication, a collection of poems
and short stories, some fact, some fiction,
some humorous and some that may bring a

tear to your eye. We hope you enjoy the variety.

'CAROUSEL' is a slim volume to dip into,
to relax with and perhaps even inspire

you to take up your own writing.

So have some fun and enjoy the ride

WRITING

By Marion Osborn

Good writing for me has myriad tints
Its sound is like endless silence so warm
A channel from the author's heart to mine
And it lives
where I sit
where I rest
where I am
Whispering softly we can share our dreams
A fountain head never running out of steam
Churning emotions unleashing bitter perfumes
Everything's possible
when imagination is stirred

THE PALS

J Dyer

It was half past eleven at night, raining and miserable as Archie Short turned into the pit yard making his way to the check office for his token which he had to wear while down the mine.

Through the half open window "118" he called and as the checker passed his token through, a voice called "Can I see you a minute Mr Short" Archie stopped, rigid, it was twenty four years ago, almost to the day and time, the same miserable weather and that same voice, repeating those exact words.

He stood inside the office door; the Manager was sitting behind the same old table, twenty four years he thought. The Manager spoke "it's about your 'marra' Archie" Archie just shook. *"WHAT", you foisted that lazy, useless, good for nothing, waste of space on to me twenty four years ago. Well I can tell you he's only skiving and he will be back shortly so don't think you can force me to take another of your misfits. I won't do it, I will see the union first"* Archie stormed off to get his pit lamp.

The Manager turned to the checker mouth open. *"WHAT the hell was all that about?"* I only wanted to ask him how old Jack Barnes was feeling you know. *"I feel guilty for sentencing old Mr Barnes to twenty four years with <u>that</u> man!"* The checker just shook his head and laughed. Archie thread his belt through the battery loops, draped the cable round his neck and sat by the cage to have a last pipe before going down, bye.

Twenty four years, he mused, it all came back, 'Jack Barnes' my partner, my 'marra'. He knew he wasn't going to like him when they met. Twenty four years of him doing everything wrong don't drill the holes here; drill them there and there! 'You want a prop here 'watch this' 'watch that' forget that' 'where did you learn mining? 'On and on! Jack Barnes just put up with it, jobs

1

were very few and he must admit Archie Short was a true miner and he felt safe with him anywhere. Six months of working together, then another bombshell for Archie. He was called into the office, *"that pit house next to you is empty now,"* said the Manager *"your marra' wants it, he has a nice wife and son, how do you feel"?* "YOUR HOUSE, *please yourself"!* said Archie, and left.

The first that 'Ada' (Archie's wife) knew of it was when he took his pick blade home. *"What is that for"* she asked. *"Jack Barnes is moving in next door!"* The two houses with their outhouses formed a sort of patio or courtyard of cement, which reached the tarmac narrow street. *"Why the pick?"* asked Ada *"I'll explain tomorrow"* said Archie.

Next morning Ada got up to find Archie measuring the forecourt and drawing a chalk line down the exact centre and now he was chipping away with his pick at the chalk to define an unmistakable, permanent division of the patio. *"WHY"?* Asked Mrs Short? *"This will save a lot of arguments when he moves in"!* Said Archie. *"You know"* said Mrs Short *"The biggest argument you ever had was with your Mother the day you were born!! And sometimes I wish you had won"!!*

Year after year it went on, Archie sat on his side of the line, Jack on his, smoking their pipes, arguing about the pit, the allotments, washing their side of the line only, going to the club 'but never together' meeting by chance. There was one thing they both agreed on, *'NEVER AGREE ON ANYTHING'*

Suddenly he came back with a jolt, eight weeks ago Jack Barnes fell ill. Archie knew this because all his name calling did not make him bite and the Doctor put him in for an operation. Ada and Ella (Jack's wife) always had got on together and Ada helped her in her trouble, but after three weeks Ella was worried about the pit. *"See Archie"* said Ada *"He won't bite"* "Won't

2

bite?, don't know about that!" said Jack's wife "But I'll pop across to the allotment anyway"

"Hello Archie" said Ella "It's about Jack's union and the rent, he says union dues are lower when sick" "That man of yours knows nothing about nothing! Never has and never will! The rules have changed, you don't have to pay anything when sick or hurt and they send someone to look after his allotment, you can't thank them cause there is a few, so don't think of it"! "That is good of them" said Jack's wife "and thanks for having me for Sunday dinner" "That's alright" said Archie "It's not as if I was doing it for him"!

Archie had secretly been going to see his 'marra' twice a week and he thought no one knew about the books and the bottles of Guinness, so a week before Jack Barnes was to be released Ada asked Archie if he was going to the club on Sunday. "Of course, wouldn't miss it" he replied.

Sunday morning came and Archie got dressed for the club "see you later" he called out. "Ok" said Ada. When he was out of sight, Ada knocked on Mrs Barnes door "come on" she said "we'll take a slow walk to the hospital".

'ARCHIE' was sitting beside Jack's bed doing what he had been doing for twenty four years with Jack Barnes 'arguing and moaning'! When their wives walked in the ward "Funny club this"!! Said Ada. Archie was fidgeting "Oh I got lost!! So I just came here" he said. Jack said nothing, but Jack's wife had plenty to say! "ARCHIE SHORT! You are the biggest liar I have ever met! Free union, free rent, ALL the union looking after his garden, you're a bloody hypocrite"!! She yelled as she walked over and placed a lingering kiss on both Jack's and Archie's lips. Archie's wife Ada did the same.

The matron who had been watching nearby came forward "Are you Mrs Short"? "Yes" said Ada, "Well" said the Matron "We *would be happy if you would prevent your husband from visiting. We think his attitude and arguments are no good for the patient*

(Mr Barnes)"

Ada Short took her gently by the arm *"Matron, if you even have a single thought of trying to stop those two idiots meeting, you will find yourself waking up in the intensive care unit!!"*

"And I will help her put you there!!" said Ella Barnes. *"Why should anyone break up such a beautiful friendship like those two IDIOTS have!!!?"*

RAMESES - SIAMESE PUSS-CAT

Vera Downes

I look like a cat, yet behave like a dog
I run like a hare and can jump like a frog
I'm elegant, proud and terribly haughty
And yet there are times I just love being naughty
I've chewed up a dolly which no longer squeeks
The hot water bottle now dribbles and leaks
And yet they still love me I'm happy to say
Coz I'm still raising hell in my own special way
Considering all these pranks of mine
Which end in such disaster
I must be just the luckiest cat
Who ever owned a master

MISSING

Hazel Dongworth

Stillness...silence
Looking...waiting

No familiar pattern
No safe sigh
No curled warmth
No soft stroke.

Movement....sounds
Meeting...living

Tabby stripes
Silky fur
Cradles hug
Comfort purr.

FOUR PENNIES AND A FARTHING WORTH OF SORRY

J Dyer

Friday night I am walking toward the token office in the pit yard. As I am not yet down the mine I do not have a token to hand in, but I do have to sign out to prove that I am alive and going home, not trapped somewhere. This is called working 'on bank' (working above ground) opposed to working 'down bye' (meaning underground).

As I am signing the register, the keeker (top deputy) puts his hand on my shoulder, "would you like an extra shift"? As I am not yet fourteen I am not allowed to work down the mine, as fifteen is the age of underground working. "Yes please" I gasp "only one day mind"! He says "come in tomorrow morning four o'clock and see deputy Cameron, you will only be inspecting the airways, not working, don't be late, alright"!

My wage was only two shillings and two pence so the extra penny farthing would come in handy.

I reckoned my father came in from the mine (not ours) at one o'clock in the morning, so he could waken me at three which would allow me ample time to walk to the pit and sign in. But oh no! I would have to have a token as I am going 'down bye'. When I got home, I gave my wages to my mother, 2s 2d, informed her excitedly of the news, the extra shift, she put the money in her purse and began to get ready to go out. She always went out about six thirty, not a word about my extra shift! Oh yes, she did say "Leave a note for your father, he will call you".

Well that night, not having a radio, I mucked about for a while then at nine o'clock I put the three kids to bed (Oh yes that was my job!) took my pants off, then went to bed myself.

Saturday Morning

Father woke me at three o'clock as I had asked on my note to
him, in fact I had written two notes, one note for him and the
other to my mother asking her for a cigarette. These two notes I
had squeezed between the brass cover and the mantelpiece,
placing them well apart.

I was sitting on the lounge cracket; (home made seat) father was
in his old armchair (courtesy of a dead neighbour) the fire was
well built up with miners coal (not free as so many think!) "I
have poured a cup of tea" dad said. I was removing my pit
stocking from my right foot. "What the hell are you doing?" he
asked. "It's on the wrong foot" I replied. You see both stockings
had holes in them and it was easier and better to double them
under in the same pit boot as before, or so I believed! Well that
was my idea.

"How long have you been smoking?" dad asked out of the blue,
it was on the tip of my tongue to say 'five foot seven' but I
declined. I was half asleep anyway and he would not have seen
the joke. "I don't smoke" I replied, as the back of my head left
his hand like a coiled spring! I realised something was amiss, he
growled, "I don't like lies, how long have you smoked"? "Not
very long" I said, I drank some tea mainly to clear my head, He
gave me a note; it was my note that I wrote to my mother,
'how'? I glanced up at the brass facing, no notes there. I was
almost ready to leave. "I have put you up a jam sandwich and a
bottle of water" he muttered why the extra shift"? After I
explained, he scared me for a while, "keep close to the deputy"!
He said, "don't lose sight of him for one second, get lost and
they will never find you. Alright"!

As I was leaving he asked, "Where is your mother"? That's it I
thought, he has flipped his lid, he had lost it. "She's in bed" I

answered as I walked out of the door. "Heyop" he called (why could he never say my name!) "I only had one 'tab' (cigarette) so I halved it, it is in your pocket!" Now I know he has gone light! I set out for the walk to the pit, which would take half an hour or more.

Reaching the yard was different, the token office, lamp cabin and pithead were all lit up unlike the daytime.

Deputy Cameron was sitting there waiting "your token number is five five one" he said "you are with me" I nodded "come on I will get you a lamp". The battery hung on my hip like a block of lead, I slipped my belt through the loops dragging my belt and pants down, I followed the deputy to the pit head. The on setter rang for the cage that lifted the safety gates as it arrived out of the gloom. The on setter opened the metal gate and we entered. The gate was shut, he rang the bell, then we were dropping like a stone, suddenly the cage stopped with a jerk, we had arrived. After getting out, "sit here" I sat "now" he said "we are going to inspect the airways from here to the 'Clara Vale' colliery, just stay with me and everything will be alright" 'Clara Vale'! I knew was miles away from our mine.

We walked for quite a while with me following very close until he suddenly held up his hand, I stopped, there was an opening to our left, "this is what I am looking for, follow me" follow you, I'm going to be more of a shadow to you than the one you have had all your life! From that spot on, it was an absolute nightmare, from that turning on I was scared almost silly, sometimes we were wriggling on our bellies, I could see the roof scraping his back as we wormed through, then we were out and you could barely see the ceiling or 'top' as he called it. Just as quickly we were slipping and sliding down a steep gradient or just as suddenly clutching and grasping climbing up a steeper hill or 'heavy' as he called it. On and on, scared out of my wits, 'lost sight of the deputy' 'get lost' I was almost riding 'pick a back' with Andy he told me to call him. Without knee pads, my knees were sore and skinned as were my hands, my back ached, my head was aching from bouncing off the 'top' as Andy called it.

Just as quickly as it had begun, Andy muttered "two canvas doors ahead," we carried on through them, lifting them up to pass. I saw railway lines "this is Clara Vale pit" he called. We were almost walking upright now. "Quarter of an hour to the shaft". Luck was not on our side, the shaft was not working Saturdays, it was another long walk to the drift entrance. Andy and me at last reached the drift entrance. We called in the token cabin to report, Mr Cameron did it for both of us being deputy. "I have to fill in a report about the airways and your conduct" he said. I looked up at him in askance "tell your dad I'm proud of you". He gave me a penny "take the bus, Clara Vale is much further to walk home". I took it and thanked him, god I was tired as I got on the bus.

Homecoming Saturday

Tiredly, but proudly, (I had been 'down bye' six and a half miles) I trudged up the back lane, knees, hands, feet, head absolutely sore. Turning in the doorway I heard a babble of voices, 'our door'. I looked up at the number, fifty eight, yes it was Edward Street, yes. Warily I climbed the back stairs stopping just inside the scullery. Although I had lived in the same street all of my life, Aunt Jenny, Aunt Annie, Etty, Uncles and Cousins had never, never, ever entered our house. We went to their places except my mother (remember I am only thirteen!) but them coming to ours! Never ever. At first all ignored me as it I wasn't there, talking across each other, questions, half answers, talking and sympathising with father, who said in his old armchair (courtesy of a dead neighbour!) and then as it by a pre-arranged signal everything was aimed at me! What time did I go to bed! Where was my mother? Did I put the bairns to bed? What time did she go? "What are you talking about"? "I always put the kids to bed"!

"Nine o'clock"! "What's matter"? I see even Uncle Charlie and Aunt Nora are here from Seaham Harbour, he's pointing to the scullery, I return to it and wait, (oh god I am tired and sore!) Uncle Charlie follows, "listen Joe" he never said 'heyop' or 'hey-oo', "I'm afraid that after you went to bed last night, your mother came back, packed her things and left"! "Did you see her"? I explained everything to him, "I'm sorry" he uttered, father never spoke or asked me anything. SORRY! They were SORRY"!! I had spent eight hours in the bowels of hell! Scared out of my wits! Legs, arms, back, skinned! Absolutely sore! More work in the future, I bring an extra penny farthing into the house! My mother and everything else goes out of the house and they have the gall to tell ME!! THAT THEY ARE SORRY!! Oh my!!

FAIRIES

J G Dyer

So you don't believe in fairies or pixies elves and gnomes
So you don't believe that fairies visit children in their homes
Well I can tell you we are real and what I say is true
Why just last night at midnight we came to visit you
When you were tucked up snug and warm, cosy in your bed
We came in through the window and flew above your head
We hovered there above you, then through the bright moonbeams
Sprinkled moon dust on your eyes to give you pleasant dreams
So when you wake each morning, look close round window frames

You may just find a sign that says, your fairies have been again.

THE FIFTH OF NOVEMBER

Ivy Brown

'Remember , remember' is what we say
When the fifth of November is on it's way
For on this day in 1605
King James 1st did survive
Because the plot to end his reign
Was fortunately all in vain
It seems that the conspirators' intent
Was to blow up him and his Parliament
But for them it all went wrong
When a secret informer came along.
The house was searched and underground
A plotter named Guy Fawkes was found
He was arrested in the cellar for what
Soon become known as the 'Gunpowder Plot'
He was eventually hanged, with another seven
It's unlikely that they went to heaven.
Now every year - come what may
We celebrate 'Guy Fawkes Day'
Parents satisfy their children's desire
By letting them see the local bonfire
For one thing they would have learned
Is that an imitation Guy Fawkes would be burned
Of course there will be fireworks too
So if you attend - let me warn you
These can be dangerous - especially the rockets,
Oh and another thing - watch your pockets
Because these days, I have no doubt
There are many more baddies about
And I'm sure they're bound to try
To get more than a 'penny for the Guy'

THE DOVE

Michael Fabb

It was Christmas Eve, about eleven o'clock on a freezing cold wet night and the rain was beginning to turn to sleet. The street was almost empty, but for a few late stragglers, the odd taxi taking merrymakers home from the pub, or the faithful on their way to church for Midnight Mass. The small slight bent figure of a young boy aged about eight with a club foot and a makeshift crutch limped slowly down the familiar street. The only clothes he was wearing were a thin threadbare jacket over an equally thin shirt, a pair of worn out tracksuit bottoms two sizes too large and turned up at the bottom and an old pair of thrown out trainers. He was wet through and shivering with the cold. He came at last to a large derelict house and went inside, it was deserted. He looked round carefully to see if he could find any discarded newspapers or cardboard, but there was nothing. So he found the corner where the staircase used to be, out of the wind and sleet, huddled himself into the corner, lying on the cold concrete floor against the two walls of the corner. 'At least he was in the dry' he thought, although you wouldn't think so, with the thin clothes that he was wearing being soaking wet. He was feeling utterly wretched, rejected and unwanted. His deformed foot was paining him again and hunger was gnawing at his empty stomach as he tried to sleep. At least he had stopped shivering now... It was then that he noticed an old man standing by him and automatically held out his hand, begging to be given something. The old man smiled sadly and putting his arm around the boy's shoulder, pulled him close as it to protect him and keep him warm. He asked the boy his name, "Noel" the boy replied, feeling better now that he had someone who was prepared to talk to him, thankful also for the warmth that seemed to radiate from the old man. "Have you any food"? He asked suddenly, but the old man shook his head. "No, I'm sorry I haven't". He paused, thinking...'Noel? Well now there's a thing' then he said "I don't suppose you know where that name came from do you?" "No" the boy replied "Where did it come from?" suddenly interested. "Well" said the old man, "some people say it was sung by the Angels the night that Jesus was born and others say that it was a hymn that was made up to celebrate Jesus being born". "Who was Jesus"? Asked the boy quietly.

"Well" continued the old man, "Jesus was born about two thousand years ago in a country called Israel. It's a very old true story and there are many versions and this is one of them. It's about a small grey dove". The old man settled himself more comfortably on the hard stone floor and told the boy this story.

"The small grey dove flew into the old stable owned by the local inn keeper. It was deserted apart from the two straggled-haired oxen who pulled the inn keeper's cart when he went to market, a goat for the milk it produced and a few sheep which could be used for food. It was a cold winters night and the oxen's breath hung heavily in the chill air. The dove perched herself on one of the dusty stone ledges, facing the stalls where the two oxen were tethered. She peered round the stable with her sharp beady bright eyes, decided that all was well and started to preen herself. It was a strange night. There was a kind of expectancy in the air. As if the world itself was holding its breath, waiting for something to happen. Something wonderful, in that ordinary, yet special place. Even the stars seemed to be bigger and brighter than ever before. Especially one that had appeared larger and closer than all the others. It was right overhead and its light seemed to be shining even more brightly as it shone through a gap in the roof, making a strange cross-like patch of light onto the floor of the stable. All of a sudden she stopped preening herself as she heard the sound of voices and the sound of a weary donkey's hooves clattered in the hard stone ground of the yard outside the stable. The animals stirred. It was the inn keeper they had heard talking, apologising to a young couple that they had no room left in the inn, indeed in the town, but he hoped that they would be comfortable here, at least it was warm and dry. He strew some more hay on the floor explained that the town was crowded with people who had to come and register their names on the census that the Roman Emperor Caesar Augustus had decreed. A lot of old nonsense many people had said, but then the Emperor's word was law since he ruled the country. The traveller said "That is why we are here also" and said no more. The inn keeper left them, leaving them two lighted lamps on stands, their orange light giving a warm glow to the whole of the stable, which in no way lessened the light from the star overhead. The dove blinked and thought how strange it all was as she sat there and watched. The man, whose name was Joseph, laid his staff against the wall and gently helped the young woman, his wife Mary, off the back of the little donkey who had dutifully carried her carefully all the way from Nazareth in Galilee to Bethlehem in Judea. Joseph laid Mary down in the deep straw at the back of the stable and covered her with a cloak while the donkey made its way into a stall and began to eat.

They were all very tired after that long and often tedious journey. Especially Mary, who was heavily pregnant and was due to give birth to a new life at any time. During the whole nine months of her pregnancy, Mary had no problems, no pains or discomfort at all, but then she and her husband both knew that the child that was to be born that night was to be someone very special, some- thing miraculous was going to happen..... The old stable suddenly felt warm and secure, as if it was being protected in someway, as indeed it was, by the Power of the Spirit that created all things. All was still and quiet, as if the very world was holding its breath.

Suddenly the woman moved and a bright light suddenly appeared, filling the dark stable with an unnaturally brilliant bright white light, so bright that no one could see a thing. A sound, as if a huge choir could be heard singing "Glory to God in the highest and Peace to people on earth". In that instant, her baby boy was born, there were no cries of pain, nothing, only a great joy of the birth itself, as her son entered the world, moving from her womb to the outside world, like someone moving from the darkest night into the light of the brightest day. The father

Joseph picked up the child and gave it to its mother; who whispered "Jesus", as they adored the child of God. They then wrapped the child in its 'swaddling clothes'. Joseph put some hay into a spare manger, put the baby Jesus into it, used it for a crib, placing it next to its mother. The donkey and the other animals all knelt on their front knees and bowed their heads before the child including the little dove, paid him homage. The little dove blinked her bright little eyes, did she really see all that she had just seen and had it all really happened? She nodded and cooing happily, closed her eyes, tucked her head under her wing and slept. The bright light in the stable slowly subsided and the lamps shone out brightly once again. Only the light from the bright star shone brightly through the crack in the roof onto the baby Jesus; All around the heads of Joseph, Mary and the baby Jesus, there seemed to be a golden glowing halo; All had become calm and peaceful once more. They all knew that this bay was destined to be someone very special. 'The Saviour of the World'... As for the little grey dove, its feathers had been turned white as snow and a voice seemed to say to her "You my little dove will be the symbol of my peace for evermore"... They all slept".

The boy looked up into the old man's eyes, smiled happily, nodded and giving a sigh, he died. As his last breath left his inert emaciated body, it formed itself into the shape of a dove. As it slowly disappeared upwards, the old man also vanished.

A few minutes later two men came into the deserted building. Searching it with powerful torches, they saw what looked like a bundle of old rags lying in the corner. They went over to investigate and found the body of the dead boy. "Better call the ambulance Bert" said one, as he bent and felt for the absent pulse "this one looks as if he's for the 'Purple annex', poor little beggar"!

Gloria, in excelsis Deo

THE SNAIL

Margot S Cooper

The sun had started to get a bit of heat in its rays, even though the calendar said January. It had beguiled the snail to venture out from the shelter of the terracotta pot. It had left a slimy sparkling trail across the brick paving. So many front gardens were now just bricks, but at least this front garden had half a plot of juicy foliage.

The next piece of terracotta he climbed gave way to disappointment, as when he reached the top expecting to find soil he only found a smooth top of more? He was on top of the milk cooler protector, but beside him a leaf tickled his antenna. He slid over the stem of the lavender bush then realised there was more to find out at this heady height. The bright green of the container conifer was too rough so he skirted around that as he felt for softer vegetation. His luck was in, as sliding over the soil he found the self sown wallflower seeds by the side of the front lobby. So lush, and look a little crack in the brick work he wiggled and slid in through the old letter box.

It was mighty warm in the enclosed sunshine behind the double glazing, but so many exciting surfaces to climb. The brown board was a smooth but rough texture and he wondered where it would lead to. His shell of tiny flecked yellow on brown just gave a camouflage effect. It was quite a steep climb as the board rested against the house wall at an acute angle of about sixty degrees. He paused and the relentless heat dried out his secretions and stuck him fast. He stayed there for the rest of the day gradually drying out and that evening it was so cold he wished he was back at ground level. The next morning the front door opened and a hand plucked the shell away from the board. He was dumped unceremoniously into the roadway, shrivelled and dead. All because the sun had teased him to be adventurous before Valentines day.

BI-LINGUAL

A Salton

It was one of those days and I'd had enough of everything. I stormed into the living room where my husband was sitting comfortably reading. That irritated me even more. So throwing down the gauntlet, I shouted "Geoffrey, I'm sick and tired of cooking, cleaning and everything else connected with this bloody house. I want to go on a holiday. Now".

He hardly looked up from the papers he was holding and said "What a good idea. Your Mother always likes to see you".

"I'm not talking about going to her in bloody Clacton, I want a real holiday, sun, sea, sand and a bit of excitement. What are you going to do about it"?

He actually looked up saying "You know full well I can't get away at this time of the year with the work I've got to do and we've also got the finals for the darts competition coming off".

"You think more of your damned darts than you do of me" I screamed as I fled the room with the final remark "I'll go on my own".

We never mentioned the subject again, so he was most surprised when I came in one afternoon after a four hour visit to our local Travel Agents clutching a wallet with all the papers describing what to me would be my dream place for two weeks.

"I've booked my holiday" I said casually. He couldn't believe that after all the years we'd been married I'd have the courage to do it. I handed the papers to him and said "That's the place, the Toledo Hotel 'on the Isla de Tabora off the coast of Spain on the Mediterranean side.

He took the papers and went through them a bit too quickly I thought to take it all in. Handing them back to me saying "Never heard of the place, but it sounds nice". We never mentioned the subject again until my air ticket and other documents turned up and it was time to go to the airport.

He never made any bones about taking me, but seemed to be most embarrassed about the whole thing and at the gate gave me a hasty kiss saying "Look after yourself" then I was through to the aircraft and suddenly realised for the first time for ages I was on my own. My thoughts "Have I done the right thing"?

All doubts left my mind as the plane came in to land at Cartagena Airport and could see what to me was the most beautiful picture of Spain down below as the full glare of the sunshine stimulated all the colours that were down there.

By the time I got onto a coach to take us to the ferry that would take me to the Island or Isla as I now liked to think of it, I felt so heady and light hearted it's a wonder no one pulled me in for a drugs test. The coach was about half full with others going to the same destination, but I didn't want company and found a seat to myself.

The hour long coach trip showed a country as I never imagined with everything so bright in the sunshine, especially after the dull and miserable weather I had left behind in the UK. It was a real tonic.

The ferry was already waiting for us at Santa Pela and over in the distance I could see the blob that others said was my Isla and I scrabbled aboard the ferry as though afraid it would go without me.

An hour's journey across the bluest of blue seas and the hotel came into focus. Standing out on the front a brilliant white among all the colourful houses that surrounded it; it looked like an oil painting.

After we docked, I rested, showered and changed to go down to dinner where I had the most sumptuous paella and fish courses that brought the pig out in me, washed down with half a bottle of wine. Something I hadn't done for years, I felt really yellow mellow.

I had to get some air, so stepping out of the hotel I became enchanted by the sight of the moon shining on the sea, turning it to quicksilver, the heavens above sparkled all over with stars, filling it with a brilliance I had never seen back home.

It was magical. I walked down to the front as though in a trance, sitting myself on a bollard just taking the scene spread out before me when my reverie was interrupted by a voice saying "Da pret- ty ladee enjoying da sennery uh? Alone uh? Alone nu good uh?"

Annoyed at being interrupted, I turned to look at the speaker, he was of stocky build with a lovely head of hair and in the light looked gipsyish, something accentuated by the shirt and trousers that in the strong moonlight I could see were yellow and green. Seeing the look on my face he said "Yer na lak me spek uh?" and he smiled.

Strong white teeth flashed at me in the light, flustered with the sight of him I said "Sorry, but you startled me!"

"So sorry lovely ladee" he said in that broken English. That and his charming manner and the frame of mind I was in at the moment he won me over from the start. He was so different from Geoffrey, although to be honest Geoffrey was far from my mind. Hadn't I come away on my own for a bit of excitement and this was it.

From that early meeting, Pedro as he called himself and myself were inseparable and I mean that literally. On that first meeting it wasn't so much the earth moved, it was more the beach trembled a bit and after that in his flat the bed moved, the table moved, the chairs moved and everything that could move, moved.

Then at the end of the week it all came to an end as he told me he had to get back to "Iz buzzness", as he called it and that was the last I saw or heard of him and the telephone number he gave me turned out to be a false one when I tried it later.

I returned home and picked up where I had left off. Geoffrey thought I was a bit withdrawn and reckoned it hadn't been a good idea me going away on my own. I differed with him there, but had to be careful not to give anything away.

The holiday was starting to diminish in my mind until one day I decided to travel to a market I'd heard about in Romford. Walking through the market - I had a shock. Over by one of the stalls stood Pedro. I started to walk over to him when suddenly he yelled out "Git yer taters here girls! Two boxes of strawberries fer a pound, ripe bananas, ripe bananas, a pound a panful!"

I turned and hurried away. My week of romance wasn't as romantic as it seemed to have been.

FIRST AND ONLY LOVE
THE MEETING

John Bartholomew

Let us go hand in hand again, as we did when we were young
Our feet were bare, our thoughts, reflected in the silly songs we sung
What happened to those virgin footprints, lost in the sands of time?
I used to admire their symmetry, yours so neat and small compared to mine

We walked to find the sun one day, as it sank into the sea
It seems we walked right into love, happily you and me
I had to laugh when you walked into the water, to show me you were brave

And nearly had hysterics when you were caught by that big wave

We strolled on many moonlit nights and oft at the break of day
We always waited eagerly waiting for the tide to ebb away
There were many secret surprises in the flotsam, on the sand
Mysterious shapes and textures, trapped in the tidal band

There was seaweed designed by Neptune scattered about the shore
We laughed and clothed ourselves in it, till we could laugh no more
That was the very first time our lips had seriously met
We stood and stared until the tears ran, how can I ever forget?

I loved you from that moment clad in your sandy dress of weed
Then we knew we were in love, as nature had decreed
Laughingly we realized we were a sight, unfit to be really seen
The ragged salty Sea King and you my lovely Mermaid Queen

Whatever happened to our footprints? Are they still there in the sands?
Will they recognise and hear us if we laugh, sing and clap our hands

Let us stand in wonderment, as we did those years gone by
Enchanted by the meeting of the sun, the land, the sea

And the meridian of the sky. (So very well met; you and I!)

EPITAPH FOR FIVE LOST SOULS

Marion Osborn

Had they really died before their killer they met
Tania, Anneli, Gemma, Paula, Annette
Sad junkies selling their bodies for the next fix
In an innocuous sounding place called Ipswich
Were these five poor lost souls the tip of the iceberg
The sorrow of the public a meaningless dirge
Will our media's spotlight all yet come to naught
Business as usual now the killer is caught
Or shall something be done about this tawdry trade
Punters who used them feel shame for the part they played

Yet these young girls like so many died long ago
And from their desolate lives had nothing to show
For the drugs that ruled them claimed them that is for sure
And while we shut our eyes there will not be a cure

MOTHER LOVE

Marion Osborn

Every Mother experiences loss
the reason being simple because
the little child on whom she doted
and all her waking thoughts devoted
grows up to be a different person
who makes her dreams go for a burton

SOOTY AND THE ASHES

J Dyer

We had a test match to play, held of course in the back lane and I was hoping to bring the 'Ashes' back to Edward Street. We had the stumps and a bat Jack had made for us out of an old barrel, courtesy of the tips and a tennis ball, courtesy of big Sep Hepple (the other Captain). The 'Ashes' were really coal dust in an old oxo tin. Suddenly, as we tossed for innings with an old token, there was a very loud "Hey op!" "Oh god; my Father".

Why "Hey op!" from him and "Hey ooo!" from her!

I had been christened and Joseph was my name. I gave the bat to Woodrow Easton "You're Captain till I get back" I said. Leaving I ran up the back stairs and into the kitchen. Father has the clothes line on the table to which he is tying long strips of rolled up newspaper to, at about two foot intervals.

Without even thinking I say, "It won't fly, far too heavy!". I stand there while he nurses his hand in his armpit, (which he has hurt clipping my left ear!) "Funny Boy" he says, "The chimney is smoking Funny Boy!". I almost say "Well! Isn't it old enough?" but I don't (thinking of my right ear). The smoke is affecting your Mother's throat and lungs. Before I can even stop myself "It wouldn't dare" I say "not her, it wouldn't dare!". Now Father is nursing his left hand and my right ear has gone BELL RINGING! There is a bottle on the table; surely he's not going to put it all in the bottle! As like a ship? He's gone nuts if he is. Then he explains to me "I've been up in the loft" he says "and taken a couple of bricks out of the chimney breast, I want you to sit in front of the fireplace and watch for the bottle coming down! Then I'll jiggle it, knocking all the soot down" he grins. I knew there was no fire lit, so he's not crazy!

"When I get on the chair" he said, "hand the things up to me". On the landing at the top of the front stairs was a table with a chair on it. As he was climbing up I was about to say "Dad it's a long drop down there!" (But then a bleeding nose would not help things much!" So I kept quiet as he disappeared into the dark loft. I pulled a chair to the fender and sat there waiting and waiting! And waiting! Suddenly I nearly died when a voice from the hearth

said "Is it there?". Shaking head to foot "No it's not here!" "I'll lower it some more and jiggle it!" said the voice. I just sat there watching. "Is it there?" GOD this is crazy. "No not here yet!" I yell. It is then that I call to him. "Dad", "yes" he says. "There is a knock at the door", "see who it is, I will wait" says Dad. I go to the door, it is Mrs Wilson "Hello Joseph, is your Dad in?" "Yes" I say. "Can I see him, I'm in a bit of trouble" Mrs Wilson says. "I'll go and get him". (Not daring to look down) I call up "Dad, Mrs Wilson is in trouble, she wants your help!". His feet show "Hold the chair". He clambers to the floor, Mrs Wilson looks really worried. "Can you help me Tim" (that's my Father). We follow her down the back stairs, along the path, then into her back yard. She shows us into her kitchen. Her unmarried Daughter Lottie is standing by the table sobbing and shaking covered in SOOT. Where she had been sitting 'legs akimbo' was a clear space in the shape of a massive shuttlecock! On the hearth were six loaf tins and two large bread rolls, waiting, rising ready for the oven, but now almost hidden in soot! The fire glow could be seen through the soot and Dad's bottle could be seen at the back like Nelsons Column.
Mrs Wilson had her head on Dad's shoulder sobbing her heart out.
'WELL' I thought. As Mrs Wilson lived directly below us and I was no good at jiggling or taking bricks out of chimneys, I would leave him to explain how the bottle got there! (If she had seen it anyway!) And how to get Mother's clothes line back out of the wrong chimney, plus I could not bear to look at Mrs Wilson's anguished face!
And my test match was a worry too.

PS. We lost the test match, Sep Hepple (Charles Atlas) had us out in ten balls.

PPS. When I got there, Sep was eight hundred and ninety five not out! (The five was for a bye) Yes, a bye is only one but this is Sep Hepple.

NO ASHES, PLENTY OF SOOT!!

THE LONDON I LOVE

Lewis Button

Joyous town sing its name aloud,
The merry throng the bustling crowd.
The salesmen who sell their wares,
Along, the crowded thoroughfares.
Magnificent buildings standing tall,
Some old, but still beloved by all.
Then the new, the changing skyline scene
The parks delight us in between.
Then in the stony palace yard
Behold the changing of the guard.
The sight this joyous majesty,
That's what London means to me.
The mixture of both the east and west
This golden site, proud of what is best.

THE LONDON I HATE

They sleep in doorways these poor folk
Who came to London and the smoke.
The drunken louts in Leicester Square,
This once sweet place we gathered there.
The black sacks of rubbish lying in the gutter
The obscene words we hear folks utter.
They take away our cities pride
Give cause for critics to deride
Dragged down by this iniquity
London's pride sunk into ignominy.

FLORAL CASCADE

Margot Cooper

Flowers say so much
Gentle or vibrant colours
Bring back memories
Happy - sad never in between
Admiration of blooms in the garden
Cultivated in regimental rows
The pride of some keen gardener
Next door the casual scattered lush greens
Could they be self sown seedlings or weeds?
The volume of spring from the ground blues yellow and white
Above canopies of pink blossom
Later heaps of confetti on the ground
The longer days of summer the deeper the shades of reds and
oranges
Autumn now the leaves join to
Paint the countryside with colour in the sunshine
The greens change to yellow and reds
As the sun lowers in the sky to bring

Winter-bare branches against the lower sun

THE OPENING DOOR

Michael Fabb

Nathaniel Stone, (Nat to his few friends) was feeling deeply depressed on that warm summers' afternoon.

He was digging a hole at the bottom of his garden, under an old Lilac tree. His hands were sore and his arms and back were aching from the unaccustomed hard labour.

He stopped to rest for a moment and looked round the garden for a moment, his eyes misty.

It was a nice garden. Old Bert who lived a few doors away came in for an hour or two once a month and kept the garden tidy for him. All in all he did a good job, considering that he was now seventy five.

Nat suddenly felt sorry for old Bert. He had been widowed some two years back and was now trying to make ends meet on his meagre pension, by doing odd jobs for the people who lived nearby. Nat thought that he must try to give him a bit more the next time he came in.

He stopped digging again as a thought struck him - he was going to have to watch his own money too. He had some savings, but not that much even though he was an accountant ... Had been an accountant, tomorrow was to be his last day. He recalled with sudden anger as he drove the spade viciously in the ground.

The brusque letter from the Managing Director 'curtly informing him that due to the economic down-turn in business, his services were no longer required'.

He had gone and complained bitterly in person to the MD who had succeeded his father into the business, forcefully reminding him that he had given the company thirty years of dedicated service and now at fifty years of age, was too old to get another post and was too young to retire. Was this the way the company showed their gratitude to their employees? It would never have happened if his father had still been there. He had more respect for his staff!

The present MD was a young man, of the new school, where time and efficiency meant money, not personalities. He was adamant Mr Nathanial Stone would have to go.

Tomorrow he would go in and clear his desk; the last surviving reminder of a lifetimes work since he had left University - now seemed to be mocking him. From now on, it would be a solitary life.

He stopped his wandering thoughts and looked down at the hole he had been so laboriously digging. Two large tears rolled down his cheeks, his chest heaved and then he broke down, sobbing uncontrollably to himself, sitting down heavily on the rustic seat under the trees, struggling unsuccessfully to control his shattered emotions.

He had not only lost his dear wife Kathleen, who had lost her fight against cancer last year after years of pain, which she had borne uncomplainingly, now he had been made redundant.

The final straw was that the day before yesterday was when his dearest and most faithful friend, his Labrador dog 'Sheba' had died in his arms. "It was old age" the Vet had said, as he carefully took the remains away to be cremated. He had returned yesterday with a small urn, which now lay at his feet.

He now had the heart-rending job of laying him in his last resting place, under the Lilac tree where he used to lay on the hot summer days to keep cool.

Nat, having recovered his composure a little, picked up the urn and placed it gently in the middle of the hole and with a heavy heart carefully filled it in.

He put his hand in his pocket and pulled out the dead dog's collar, removed the engraved tag that he had bought for her when she was a puppy. He stood and looked again at the tag, pain again crossing his face as he recalled the many pleasant hours they had spent together.

He hung the collar on a branch of the Lilac tree. He would get old Bert to finish the job properly the next time he came in. He would get a small headstone with an inscribed brass plaque on it.

As for 'Sheba's' tag, he would put that in a safe place as a reminder, as if he needed it, of a good and faithful friend.

He walked slowly back to the house, now strangely quiet and empty. He sat down in his favourite chair, put the tag on the occasional table next to him and automatically dropped his hand to fondle his dog's ears ... He pulled himself up short feeling guilty. Before he had time to do anything else, the telephone rang. He picked it up and said "Hello, Nathaniel Stone here". "Ah, good afternoon Mister Stone", said the disembodied voice cheerfully. "I'm Father Ronald Jackson of St Boniface's Roman Catholic Church just down the road from you, Bert your gardener put me on to you. You are an Accountant I believe?" "Yes" said Nat dully. "Well, the chap who normally does our books ... The priest rattled on ... Nat listened to his request and arranged to meet the priest that evening and put the telephone back on the hook.

He suddenly gave a small sad smile as he recalled the line 'as one door closes, another one opens'.

THE SMILE

J G Dyer

Trees and flowers loan their beauty to the poets' pen
Songsters sing their praises to the valley and the dell
The dawn begins it's loveliness with early morning dew
Could I extol it's virtues less than I begin with you
The swallows light the sky larks song the humming of the bee
Such wondrous sounds we hearken to such grace the world to see
This land so full of beauty that song and verse beguile
Words cannot tell nor song portray the magic of a smile

SOUNDS OF THE DAY

A Salton

Deep dark of early morning hours
No Moon to cast its mellow glow
When golden silence is deafening
Until broken by a Foxes cry
Or the faint rustle of Nocturn's
Going about their shadowy business
As Earth awaits Sol's return
To dissolve the blackness that
Diluted by ever strengthening light
Submits to that greater power
And moves on
To cast its shadows over pastures new
The great awakening starts
Before full light returns
A Birdsong cacophony
Alarm clocks ringing out annoying tones
Reminding owners another day is here.
Whispering along high in the sky
Silver birds ride the skyways
Home again from foreign shores.
Cars roar their way to unknown destinations
Driven by early waking drivers
Eager to get to where ever
As quickly as possible.
Vying for their share of road
Motorcycle engines shatter the air
As they monopolise spaces
Between traffic lines.
Adult footsteps hurrying, scurrying,
Must get to work on time.
Children's voices nattering and chattering
On the way to School
For another round of education.
So the day goes on
Full of noise that we hardly notice
Until Sol has had his day
And the dark of night
Overcomes him once again

THE BROODING WOOD

John Bartholomew

The wayward wind is as devious as a running Fox
Twisting and turning and wriggling this way and that
Cascading scent and sound as the solo Cuckoo mocks
The predatory amusing antics of a feral Cat

The Squirrel from their larders helps the trees to grow
While the Jay, Crow and Jackdaw argue all the time
Other denizens of the canopy flitter to and fro
Visiting courting, feeding in the Hornbeam, Oak and Lime

Darkness cloaks other acts of hunting and mating
Alas the steady stalk of a killer, wherein death means life
Power of patience and practiced cunning always waiting
Inherited instinct and the will to live, is forever rife

The moon goes down the sun comes up in a scene serene
Baby Rabbits and their parents gambol feed and play
Day repaints rainbow colours and many shades of green
The wise old Owl and twittering Bat seem to fade away

Weasel and Stoat very soon make their mandatory kill
Carrion Crow and Magpie vie fiercely for their share
Predation is inherited and a very well practiced skill
Most times the vagaries of life are never fair

So many living creatures depend upon the land
Snakes, Beetles, Flies and Man just to name a few
Red in tooth and claw as Nature's Laws demand
Doubtless the victims of predation have a different view

The brooding wood, in sunlight; at touch of paradise
In darkness a fearful clutch of ancestral mystery
Especially when the Owls are chasing flying Mice
Then Premier Man is apt to retire gracefully

Live, eat and be merry
For some to live some must die

The Spider told the Fly

LIVING IN MY HEAD

Lewis Button

My name is Aiden. I live within my head where I am alright. I do get frustrated though, it is mainly when people do not understand me. I try my best to be patient, but sometimes I have to shout and scream. Some people took me and my classmates to the theatre to see what they call a pantomime. I really wanted to go there as my friends were all so excited to see the actors, but I do have this fear of people dressing up in strange clothes. I do not know why, it just makes my head spin. When we got to the theatre my teacher, Miss Barley said to this man, "hold Aidens hand Lew", this I did and I said not go in, he smiled and nodded and I just held his hand and shook my head. I was beginning to panic, I could not face going in, my stomach churned I just shook my head, but no one knows how scared I am, no one understands. My teacher parked the coach and came back smiling. She smiles a lot my teacher Miss Barley. She has a kind smile, but I still feel miserable, Not go in, I kept saying, not go in.
I saw all of my friends inside all happy all smiling and I wanted to be with them, but my legs would not go in. I shook my head, why don't they understand, me not go in. Suddenly I went in, I don't know how, but I was standing in the theatre with my classmates. A bell rang, a man shouted take your seats, the show will start in five minutes, I shook and cried, shook and cried, not go in. An old man with a funny waistcoat said to my Miss Barley, take the boy up the stairs to the back of the auditorium, he might be better there. So I went up the stairs and looked at the performers dancing and singing, this must be the pantomime I thought. I still would not go in, but peeked through the curtains. The man in the funny waistcoat said to Miss Barley I'll save you two seats at the back. But I would not go in, all the children laughed and sang and cheered. I did so want to be with them, but couldn't then Miss Barley said "I'm tired Aiden, I must sit down" and sat in one of the seats. I felt tired too, but I could not go in,

but suddenly Miss Barley looked up and I was sitting right there next to her and I waived to all of my friends in the front rows.

The interval came and Lew and another lady called Deep handed out sweets and drinks and I came down and sat with my friends. The music was lovely, the girls were so pretty and they danced and sang and funny men made us laugh. I told Lew I like this, I like this very much. I booed when the Ugly men started on poor Cinderella, it was good. Then there were two men on the stage singing a song that we sing at school called 'I am the Music Man'. When they got to the part that was I'm the music man, I am a Dam Buster, he put his arms out like an aeroplane and spun around. I pushed past Lew and he tried to stop me, but I was too quick. He thought I was going out the door, but I started dancing in the aisles, down the steps singing as I went with my arms outstretched "I'm the music man", I like this pantomime. I don't know why, but Lew was crying and so was Deep. I think I like this pantomime, I'll come again, "next year" said Lew.

FOREWORD, FOREWARNED!

John Rogers

There is a wealth of anecdotal experience here, they will no doubt cause you to smile and even chuckle to yourself as you recognize some of the incidents you or those close to you have gone through.

This in itself proves that the subscribers are very ordinary people, capable of smiling or even shedding the odd tear over every day occurrences?

This in itself creates the Human Factor, which will, we hope, give you memorable pleasure.

A DAY IN THE LIFE OF A NOBODY

Marion Osborn

I am a nobody - a person of no importance

I hang between two Worlds waiting for a soul to inhabit

A life to take-up

A fate to redeem

A hurt to atone

A lesson to learn

I cry for forgiveness. I wait. I am afraid, but I do not know
of what.

I don't want to find out, so I fill my mind with other things

Which seem to be of such pressing importance

So that I myself seem of no importance

And I am still a nobody - and everyday is the same.

IT'S PARTY TIME

Ivy Brown

If you're feeling hale and hearty
Why not hold a garden party?
I'm sure you'll have lots of fun
Entertaining in the sun.
So start handing out invitations
To your friends and relations
Then think about the food and drink
Will it be afternoon - do you think?
There is a difference that this makes
Because then you'll need lots of creamy cakes
But if it's to be an evening 'do'
You could have a barbeque
You'll need a table, lots of seating
And a marquee would take some beating
As, I don't need to explain
It could suddenly pour with rain
Not good for ladies in party dresses
Or those protective of their tresses
The men won't care, so I hear
Unless, of course, it spoils their beer
Don't forget the lawn needs mowing
And probably the weeds need hoeing
Remember too, to trim the flowers
All this work will take you hours
Music too, that's another thing
For party folk love to sing
And dance - of course that is partly
Why they are keen to attend a party
Some will perform with karaoke
And others do the Hokey Kokey
To entertain the kids that some will bring
A Bouncy castle is just the thing
Talking of castles, don't be too keen
And put on airs, as if you were Queen
I hope it all goes successfully
Will you be inviting me?

MARKET DAY

A Salton

"Sing Hey, sing hey, for it's Market Day. Come Lads and Lassies hasten away". It's funny, but that song always goes through my mind when I'm on the rickety old bus that takes us to the market at Fletton -on- the-Squale. It's still the only transport we have in this forgotten area and it's Amos Longbottom we have to thank that we have it.

He's the owner/driver of the bus that does the journey from our village to Fletton, Monday to Friday twice a day, there and back without fail, whatever the weather. The only time he missed was when he had the cheek to go down with Flu. That was five years ago, but it's still talked about as 'Greenstock's days of isolation'. Anyway, back to what I was saying. As you can guess I'm on the bus along with a crowd of locals and passengers we've picked up along the scenic route that is the way to Fletton. Through the leafy lanes we make our way. The view over the Squale Valley that for anyone who loves the countryside like myself it's Heaven.

It's a good social occasion as the villagers get to together and on the journey there's always a lot of banter between the women and Amos the driver takes a lot of stick, but always gives as good as he gets.

On this trip I couldn't join in the fun as I had Mrs Baggage the village gossip sitting alongside me. She blasted my ears telling me what was wrong with her husband Alf and I swear she quoted the whole of a medical dictionary at me all the way there.

Coming into Fletton is always an interesting sight as the houses go back to the eighteenth century and there's so many of them there with beams and painted plaster in between that are unique in their way. The mullion windows and roofs seem to show the weight of the centuries as they sag and twist in gentle contortions to add to the character of the buildings they still manage to keep waterproof.

The bus pulled in to its final stop outside the Guildhall such an imposing building that now really looks its age and I like to go inside and savour the musty smell of it all and to tread the wooden staircase that winds up to the rooms above and to walk on the wooden floors, so well worn in places where over those years so many feet had trodden and helped to scuff the marks deeper and deeper.

We made our way to the back of the Guildhall where a large square is taken up by the many stalls making up the Wednesday Market. It was already bustling with the eager crowd of erstwhile shoppers who peered, handled and examined the contents of the stalls and some even made a purchase.

The noises so typical of a market with the buzz of the crowd and the cries of the stall holders that rose above all others, with musicians dotted around making their different brands of music creating a good atmosphere and the general hub-bub adding a gaiety to the whole happy panorama, gives me the feeling I want to get amongst it.

The first stall sold food and the smells of new baked bread, cooked meats and a variety of cheeses wafted around me tantalising my taste buds, but at the time there was a bunch of people trying to get served so I carried on inspecting clothes stalls and those selling general bric-a-brac.

After pushing through the men crowding around one stall, I found myself looking at things I didn't have a clue about from hammers to all sorts of electrical bits and pieces and I got away from there quickly leaving the men trying to think what they would find useful if they bought it.

I was out in the press of bodies again, trying not to walk over small children who were not always obvious and not always holding onto a parent's hand. Practically all the stalls had been at the market for as many years as I can remember, but on this occasion a newcomer had appeared, his stall a mass of jewellery and gold objects winking and glinting in the sunlight that seemed to concentrate on his wares. I had to stop and admire the objects that lay spread out and they seemed to hold me in a spell of admiration. I looked them over and began to pick up different pieces to examine them.

The stall holder watched me as I picked up gem set pieces one after the other and laid them down. Then I went on to the gold items that positively glowed in the sunlight and picked up a really heavy looking bracelet that positively sparkled on its high points.

The stall holder spoke up, "Lovely piece that bracelet is lady, 22 carat gold it be. Look at the thickness of all the gold that's been worked into it, you can tell by the weight that it's a classy bit of bling".

It did feel heavy as I held it and it was so chunky and delightful that I ventured, "How much is it?"

He looked at me replying, "That bracelet usually sells at over a £1,000, but today and just for you I'll let it go for £300".

I stood looking at it and said, "That's a bit too much for me" and reluctantly I laid it back in its place.

"If that's too much for you," he said, "I'll give you a special price £280, that's as far as I can go".

I picked it up again and the weight of it felt really good and that decided me, "OK" I said, "I'll take it, but I've got to go down to the bank and get some money out".

"No problem," he said "I'll put it to one side for you".

I rushed off to the High Street and found a cash machine, withdrew the amount of money I wanted and dashed back for my bargain.

He was putting his stuff away by the time I got back, but I handed him the £280 which he stuffed straight into his pocket and said, "You look an honest little lady, so I won't bother to count it" and handed me my bracelet that he'd wrapped up and placed into a bag.

I had to run off myself as I didn't want to miss the bus back home. I had to give the food stall a miss, but I wasn't worried, I wanted to have a good look at my purchase on the bus.

Once seated, I examined my bracelet. It didn't look quite so bright and sparkly in the dreary light in the bus, but I was so pleased with my bargain, so instead of putting it back in the bag I fastened it on my wrist and it looked real good.

After I got home I couldn't take my eyes off it and never took it off when I went to bed. I awoke in the morning and went to the bathroom to carry out my ablutions and before I started to shower I removed my bracelet.

Then shock and horror, the gold had given me an allergy, as where the bracelet had been round my wrist the skin had turned green. I could never wear gold again.

THE BUILDERS' GARDEN

Hazel Dongworth

In the time it took
the orange lilies to open
the new bathroom had unfurled

In the time it took
the red Hibiscus to blaze

the new kitchen had bloomed.

In the time it took
the blue Agapanthus to unfold
the house walls flowered

By the time
the Michaelmas daisies came out

the builders had gone.

NO GOODBYES

John Bartholomew

Look not for me when I have gone
For I will not be there
Having lived this life just for fun

I could be anywhere

When at times you think of me
If such reflections make you smile
One person in your memory
I will stay with you a little while

In secret thoughts you will find
Life does not last over long
You remain forever in my mind
Like a favourite melodious song

Those fond memories will remain
Beside thoughts of Kith and Kin
Of infinite joy and a mite of pain
To love each other is not a sin

I will jog your memory
Time alone will decide your fate
You will never be quite rid of me
Seek me by Life's exit gate

Friends are there for you to meet
Yes, life may end in sobs and sighs
Erstwhile rivals as well to greet
For us there are no goodbyes.

ROMANCE. THE CHAT UP

Lewis Button

Romance with me, come dance with me
Go on baby take a chance with me.

Love me true, please love me do
There's no one in the world but me and you.

Given time, you will be mine
Our tangled bodies will entwine.

It's our first date, I just can't wait,
You know you're destined to be my mate.

I'll take this vow, that years from now,
Our love will grow I do not know how.

When we kissed, you did not resist
You had seven Vodkas so perhaps you're pissed.

I'll sing you songs and right your wrongs,
This fine romance to us belongs.

REAL LIFE

Ivy Brown

Jane was clearing up after breakfast when she heard the squeal. "He's back," she cried. I'm going upstairs, I can see better from up there. "Don't let them see you," said Barry, "you'll upset them".

"He's brought her some food," Jane told him when she came back downstairs. "I was wondering if I should give them something to eat".

Barry groaned. His wife discovered this new interest twenty four hours ago and already she was obsessed. He dreaded to think how long it would go on.

The phone rang. Jane went to answer it while Barry got ready for work.

In a while they met up again. Noticing the gloomy look on Jane's face, he remarked: "Don't tell me, that was your sister, wasn't it?" Jane nodded. "She's in a right state. Derek's walked out again. They had a row last night and he hit her. I doubt if he's come back this time. I think she should start divorce proceedings. I asked her to come to lunch so that we can talk things over." Grateful that he wouldn't be around, Barry kissed her cheek and headed towards the front door. Then a thought struck him.

"Isn't your friend's divorce due soon?" "Yes, they're due in court today. By all accounts it's going to be rather messy".

Jane closed the door behind her man and went back upstairs. Would she be able to deal with her sister's depression? Should she mention divorce?

She walked sadly to the bedroom window and shook her head in disbelief as she looked again at the scene that had been holding her attention. Cooing had begun. "Why", she wondered "can't all the couples I know be as devoted to each other as the two Wood pigeons nesting in our neighbour's tree?"

By Lewis Button

Wouldn't it be wonderfully good
If everyone had clean water and food
If we did not judge people by their religion or race
The way they spoke or of accents trace
Perhaps all religions should be banned
Perhaps then peace would reign over the land
The price of essentials should be governed by all
And no longer to be summoned by bugle call
If everyone had the same colour skin
No battles to fight no wars to win
No Zenaphobia therein to divide us all
No domination with tyrants' words to enthral
If you think that this is a forlorn quest
Try the word of love instead of detest.
The world is our temple to be our aim

Do good to one another for each is the same.

WATER UNDER THE BRIDGE

J G Dyer

Much water flows past the embankment much more will flow back again
I wonder how much did flow past this morning I know that it really did rain
I'm sure that it will rain tomorrow because I have heard people say
It always will rain on a Sunday if someone goes out for the day
On Saturday morning take notice because very few people will know
Past London Bridge and Embankment, just how much water will flow
But if you really can find out, I mean to the last flowing drop
Send it to him on the Tele cause his weather is always a flop
Before you all laugh at my forecast, all those who think it absurd
Just listen to him on the Tele, that fellow who gives out the word

POLISHING

Marion Osborn

"4, and I polished off every man-jack of them too!"

Leone stared at the little old lady in some surprise. Surely she couldn't mean what she thought she did. After all, she had only asked her if she'd ever been married and when she'd said "yes" and added "more than once", Leone had responded in all innocence. "How many times was that then?"

Leone was a journalist sent round by her editor to interview Dot because of her lovely large garden, which she tended herself and at 88, this was no mean achievement. But what made her garden extra special, was that she claimed to have more than 200 garden gnomes dotted around it and as she'd wandered around Dot's garden with her, she'd been asking questions to fill in a background to her story together with photographs. To Leone's amazement every gnome and they were all so individual, had a name and they made the garden entertaining as well as beautiful. The old lady laughed at Leone's reaction to her own response and said, "Oh, you think I meant that I did them in? Well, not in the way you mean". "Do tell!" responded Leone enthusiastically, thinking that this rather boring assignment had the makings of a much more interesting story.

"Well, going back to my first husband Willie, I married him during the war. Spitfire pilot he was. Only 16 I was, but I couldn't cook for toffees. I did try and I made him a lovely meat pie before he went on his last flight. I didn't realise the meat was off did I? so while he was on a mission over Germany, he was sick as a dog and crashed. They heard him on the radio back at base saying he felt awful bad. Lovely he was. I felt really guilty about him. Took me till after the war to get over that, it did".

"Was that when you got married again?" Leone asked, after making sure there was enough tape in her recorder.

"Yes. Mind you he was a lot different to Willie. Right toe-rag he was. Proper Jack the lad, if you know what I mean. Always in trouble and no mistake, but had never been inside. He was the father of my 2 boys. He was the one who did the Bootle Street job." She looked at Leone for a reaction, but it was obvious that she had never heard of it, so she went on. "I suppose you're too young to remember it. They got away with £10 million they did. Not that I ever saw a penny of it. Cleared off to Basingstoke with his fancy woman to live the life of O'Riley. So I put him away" she cackled. "He never knew it was me. Got 30 years he did. He only served 7. I knew he wouldn't last long inside. Never could stand being cooped up he couldn't".

"You don't seem to have been very lucky in your choice of men. What happened to the next one?"

"Oh him! He was an illegal immigrant. Mum had passed away by then and left me her house. I took him in as a lodger. He was alright at first. Couldn't do enough for me. Decorated the house from top to bottom he did. So I married him. Then he turned right lazy. Packed his job in and thought he could live off the fat of the land. So I soon put paid to his game." "What did you do?" Leone asked eagerly.

"Put him away to the authorities and they packed him off to his own country. So I divorced him for desertion," Leone struggled to keep herself from laughing. "You were a bit of a girl weren't you! So what happened to the last one?"

"He ran a garden centre and that's where I got all my darling gnomes. Truth be known that's why I married him, but after we were married, he wouldn't let me have anymore, said I was eating into all his profits. Tight fisted scum-bag and in the end my darling gnomes did for him." "How did they do that?" Leone was puzzled.

"Oh, when he came home drunk one night, he fell over Joe who I'd moved into a different position and split his head open on Fred. Two of my favourite gnomes they are. Luckily he didn't damage the little darlings. Anyway, in the morning I found him dead as a door-nail."

"How sad!" exclaimed Leone. "So now you're on your own?"

"No I'm not, I've got my gnomes haven't I? They cheer me up and never answer me back and mean more to me than all of my old men put together!"

STRESS

Lewis Button

Do you get stress? Your head's in a mess.
Which way to turn? Your headaches burn
You can't think straight always running late
Panic sets in, head's in a spin
Can't get to sleep, you've appointments to keep
Will it ever end, going round the bend?
Awake all night, this can't be right.
Night and day, you have lost your way.
Filled in your form, there'll be no storm
Just relax; you've paid your tax.
Was it in time? It's so sublime.
Why do I fret? They won't ring yet
31st of Jan, that bloody tax man
He'll have your guts, Oh tell him nuts.
Now a word to the wise, just close your eyes,
And settle down in bed, you could be dead.
Everything's on top, Will it ever stop
Why fret and worry? There's too much hurry.
So just slow down, wipe away that frown.
But when you're broke it's no blooming joke
Tell 'em you'll pay, maybe one fine day.

SMOKE AND FIRE

A Salton

Dad came in from work one night a bit livelier than usual. He started to speak. That was unusual. "It's going to be a lovely weekend according to the forecast"and then with a newfound twang in his voice he said "We'll have a Bar-be"!

I thought he should never have watched that programme on Australia last week, but all of us kids gave shouts of approval that brought a pleased self-righteous grin all over his face until Mum said scathingly, "A barbecue?". Trust her to say it correctly. "If you think I'm going to sweat over a hot charcoal fire cooking burgers and sausages old man you're mistaken".
The smile went off of Dad's face as he said, "Don't worry my love; I'm going to do the cooking". "You're going to do what?" said an unbelieving Mum. "You couldn't boil a bleeding egg and you're the man who thought Cock-a-leeky was some sort of incontinence in men. Anyway, you haven't got a barbecue."
Before she could carry on any further Dad chipped in saying,"Oh yes I have. Fred at work had one to sell, so I bought it from him. It only cost a fiver. It's outside in me van".
Mum, to be right, said, "You haven't got any fuel nor food to cook on it have you?" "I'll get it in Tesco's on Friday on the way home," he said. True to his word he came in loaded with the bits he thought necessary. Charcoal stuff, enough fire-lighting liquid to keep a power station going for a fortnight and Mum seeing all the food he unpacked muttered, "We'll never eat all that".
Saturday came, it was a lovely day and we were all out in the garden to enjoy the weather and most of all to see Dad operate his culinary skills on the Bar-be, but as it turned out he needed just a bit more skill than that.
You could see he was quite proud of his Bar-be. It was like a large food trolley on wheels and then he moved it up near a fence. Then filled the fire tray up with the charcoal stuff. Then

like Ainsley Herriot, he picked up a bottle, undid the top, said, "A little drop of Freddy Fuel" and poured lighting fuel over the charcoal.

He struck a match and put it to the charcoal. It burnt down to his fingers, but there was no expected burst of flames, only a burst of language. He sucked his burnt fingers and stood looking. Then instructed Benjy to get him an old newspaper. Benjy scuttled off and speedily returned with yesterday's 'Sun'.

Dad took the paper, peeled off a few sheets, rolled them up a bit and thrust them under the charcoal, then applied the match. The paper flared and the fuel lit up. Flames spread right across the Bar-be and with them a cloud of white smoke that the wind carried over the fence into the garden next door.

From there came the sound of a door opening and a voice of Mrs Grufalus complaining about inconsiderate neighbours making all that smoke when decent people had their washing hanging out. Suddenly the smoke stopped. Dad looked anxiously at the charcoal bed. He peered into its depths. Nothing seemed to be happening. As he bent over the tray he picked up another bottle of fuel and poured the contents onto the tray.

Smoke and flame belched up enveloping Dad who staggered back with singed hair, eyebrows and even eyelashes and a face that looked as if he'd been out in the sun all day. I could have warmed my hands on it. Mum with quick thinking opened up a bottle of lemonade and poured it all over his head.

We all stood around Dad asking if he was all right. He stood in shock until suddenly Jenni screamed and pointed to the Barby where a big column of smoke and flames flared up, the fence being dry and near the Bar-be was burning away and speedily moving all along its length.

A fire engine's siren could be heard in the distance getting nearer. One of our other neighbours had seen the smoke and phoned for the fire brigade. The siren stopped and Mum rushed to the door and shortly after half a dozen firemen came charging into the garden with extinguishers that covered everything including all our food with foam. The quickly put out the blaze and went on their way.

We sat there in some sort of shock surveying the damage. Mrs Grufalus came storming out of her house raging about how we'd ruined her washing and worse of all destroyed her fence and she finished up having a go at everyone and with a final, "I hope you're going to replace that sodding fence you've cremated!" She went back indoors.

Eventually hunger overtook us as the food we were depending on was ruined, so Mum sent out for fish and chips. Back indoors, Dad who'd mumbled about the skin on his face being so tight he thought it might crack, sat rigid in his chair like some Red Indian Chief, his face as immobile as a Sitting Bull, then Mum started on him.

All in one breath she harangued him about the mess the firemen had trodden through her home, was Dad some idiot who didn't know how to light a simple fire, how were they to pay for a new fence and as sure as God was in his Heaven, never again would she ever allow a barbecue to be lit in this house.

Anyway, a new fence has been ordered. Mrs Grufalus still doesn't speak to us. Mum got the old Iron Man to take the barbecue away. Dad is sitting around, his face smothered with anti-burn ointment and is showing some improvement now, but he will never be allowed to forget his attempts at a Bar-be and to rub it in even more, Mum went shopping and on her return handed Dad a gift-wrapped package saying, "this is a reminder for you". Dad tore at the paper trying not to move his face muscles too much as he said through puckered up lips,"What's this?". He revealed a small well dressed doll. Mum in a scornful tone said "That's the last Barbie that ever comes into this house. Get it."

PARTY II *THE CURE*

By Lewis Button

Soon they were wed in Barkingside
The callow youth and his pregnant bride.
The reception in a local pub
Her Mum provided all the grub
There was ale, champagne and whisky too.
They sang and danced the whole night through

His best man told loads of jokes
Of things they did as younger blokes.
Her Nan kept shouting what was that
Her Dad said "Listen you deaf old bat."

Time to go at end of day
Friends all cheered them on their way.
To a honeymoon on the Isle of Man
In a boarding house run by his old Gran
They could only stay for just one week
In the bed with a constant creak.

Back home to their one room flat.
Where baby came and a tabby cat
He worked eight hours every day
And gave his wife all his pay

Once a week out with the lads
Now most of them were also Dads
Weekends he took her to the club
Made a change from the local pub.

They lived out their lives of drudgery
The cure for Romance, Matrimony.

THE WELL END

Michael Fabb

The young woman suddenly sat bolt upright in the bed she had
been laying on; something had woken her.
She cast her mind back in a vain effort to remember where she
was.
Then slowly her thoughts cleared and it all came back to her with
a rush.
Except, how on earth did she come to be lying there stark naked,
in a strange bed.
She remembered that she had agreed to go out to dinner with the
smart young man she knew as Tony, whom she had met only
once before in the office where she worked for a large multi
national insurance company.
The young man had come in to see Mr Smyley she remembered,
with his piercing light grey eyes, who had inveigled her to go out
on a dinner date with him the following night.
She had hesitated, but for a moment, before agreeing to accompa-
ny him.
After all, it is not very often a lonely single girl gets asked out to
dinner.
She arranged for him to pick her up at seven o'clock from her
small double-roomed flat.
Tony had taken her to a very select and expensive restaurant deep
in the heart of the rural countryside, catering for small and select
clientele, but he had seemed strangely ill at ease.
After dinner she was feeling very sleepy and had fallen asleep in
the car.
Little knowing he had dropped a knock-out tablet into her drink;
She froze as she heard the creak of someone coming stealthily up
the stairs.
The soft foot falls stopped outside her door.
As a cloud was blown clear of the moon, a shaft of moonlight fell
across half of the door and the wall.

She gasped in fear as she saw the bedroom door-latch slowly starting to rise. The old door creaked as it slowly opened.

Sheila stared as if mesmerised, as a tall dark figure stood framed in the doorway. It was Tony.

She started to relax and was about to speak, when with two quick strides he reached her and thrust a bag over her head and quickly pinioned her arms and legs with some cord he pulled from his pocket.

Sheila was screaming by now, but her cries were hardly audible inside that thick leather-lined felt bag. He picked her up bodily and carried her downstairs into the yard and there he dropped her, not onto the ground as she expected, but into space.

She plunged down into that dark, deep, wetness of the old well, her horror giving way to a terrible fear as the freezing cold waters closed over her head.

Jasper Cleethorps stood there for a few minutes, listening to the girl's struggles and then silence.

Replacing the cover over the well, he removed his overalls and gloves and threw them on the fire that he had left burning in the yard.

Then, climbing into his car, he drove off.

The A127 Serial Killer had struck again.

MESSAGE TO A GRANDSON

Lewis Button

I'll take you back to my young days
of different dreams and other ways
I'd like to open up your eyes
Of my youth with thoughts so wise.
Like you I thought I knew it all
We all thought thus as life did call.
Young man, think on. About your dream
things you get are not as they seem.
So go young man and do your best,
And travel well, fulfil your quest.
One life you have, it's not a game,
but enjoy it well just the same.
Hard knocks may come in your life's span
live, love and laugh and be a man.
Who knows in life what you'll achieve
So always do what you believe.
And when you're old think of me,
remember me well, my only plea.
With love, these thoughts I give to you
always to thyself be true.

LOCK, STOCK AND BARREL

A Salton

Sir Francis Poncette Plantagnet De-Vere was a worried knight. He was off to the Crusades for two years, but was loathe to leave his beloved Lady Jane behind, although she had sworn an oath in their bed only the night before that she would remain true to him, but worrying doubts were in his mind. There were so many knavish men around who would be keen to take advantage during his absence.

He pondered on the question. What was a knight to do when he leaves a lusty woman on her own, unattended for two years?

The night watchman provided the answer as he did a bit of advertising on the side and after his usual cry of "It's six o'clock and all's well", he announced the local blacksmith was doing a special deal on made-to-measure chastity belts with 10% off for Crusaders.

The belts were guaranteed safe as each was fitted with its own special individual lock that he defied anyone to be able to open without its very own key.

Although Lady Jane wasn't keen on the idea, he cajoled her into having a fitting to really prove her undying love for him as promised and it was that which clinched it, not that if she didn't, he would stop her allowance of ten guineas a year.

So measurements were taken, the belt made and fitted, pulled in tightly round her stomach as it was made deliberately small so it couldn't be slipped off.

Sir Francis tested the key a few times, more to make the most of the time that was left to him and that the robust lock worked perfectly smoothly and was all that had been promised. Then donning his armour and with his page's assistance, he got onto his horse and with a flourish of his lance he was off to the Crusades mind content.

He hadn't been away long when doubts crept into Lady Jane's mind. How did she ever agree to wear such an unwieldy,

uncomfortable contraption, she must have been mad.
Summoning the blacksmith to her manor, she demanded he produce a second key from the stock he must be holding, but was dismayed to hear there were no spares. The only key was the one Sir Francis possessed and as all the locks he'd made were so different, it wasn't possible to make another.

The situation worsened for her as she was getting the eye from various young men who she studiously ignored, until she came up against one Thomas Termigant in whom she found an immediate attraction, as he was to her.

It wasn't long before they endeavoured to become lovers, but were frustrated in their attempts by the fiendish belt.

Thomas tried every way he could to open the lock, hairpins, pick locks and as a last resort a hammer and chisel, but this caused Lady Jane too much pain and the lock never budged, remaining as fast as ever.

He smothered her waist with best goose fat and she wiggled about. She sucked her stomach in and went into bone-cracking contortions trying to shed that restricting belt, but the belt remained intact.

Time was running out fast and becoming desperate, she decided she would have to lose a lot of the weight that adorned her body to try to slip out of it, but there was only so much hunger she could tolerate and the process was deadly slow. As the months went by her body mass diminished, but the damned belt refused to come off. She was only half the woman she was when at last the belt slid down to the floor, but the fates were against the pair as it so happened that poor Thomas wasn't around as he had been sent away across country on an errand for the King that would take weeks. So all her efforts were in vain.

But worse was to come as a messenger arrived bearing news that Sir Francis was on his way back.

In a panic that she would be found without the belt on and knowing it would never stay on her now thin body, she decided the only way out was to reverse the situation and start eating plenty of food again. So without more ado she tucked into all the food she could until she had to get back into the torturous device before her hips got any thicker.

She received another message that his Lordship was only days' away, so cramming food down faster than ever before, she got fatter and fatter until as someone remarked she looked like a barrel. By this time the belt was so tight on her it was embedded in her flesh.

The day came when with a clatter of horse's hooves in the courtyard and a recognised voice shouted for his Page "To un-horse him", Sir Francis had returned.

Out of his armour, he strode into the manor house calling for his Lady. She appeared, he gave a roar of approval slapping his thigh as he said "My oh my, you have made yourself into a comely buxom wench in my absence."

"Oh my Lord," she said piously, "I'm so pleased to see you. Release me if you will from this perfidious belt that is intent on ruining my flesh."

"Belt, belt," muttered Sir Francis clearly puzzled. "What belt?" Lady Jane lifted her gown high. "Why this of course", she said pointing to the metal covering her nether regions.

"Oh that!" said Sir Francis.

"Have you got the key to unlock it and free me from this monstrosity?" screamed Lady Jane. "Key?" he queried. A few minutes passed "Oh yes" he said. "I remember now, I forgot to take it with me. I left it on the mantle shelf."

"My poor Lady!" he exclaimed as she fell to the floor in a dead faint.

THE THAMES, CONTRASTS

Dirty old river they once said,
But it brought us our daily bread.
Once alive, with trade from the sea.
It was our Nation's artery.
The docks Prince Albert, George V and St Catherine,
And so many more with names entwine.
Proud dockers and the stevedores
Unloaded goods upon our shores.

What German bombers could not shut down,
Were closed by accountants surly frown.
Fascist hoards with stamping feet
Were in Cable Street put in retreat
By dockers saying," Go no step more",
And Moseley was shown the closed door.

Now once where men worked day and nights
Coffee bars and hotels neon lights
And swell apartments the banks do grace.
No room for workers in this place.
The houses built for returning heroes
Are sold for tens and several zeros.

There stand the skyscraper office blocks
That have taken the place of docks.
For truth to tell we've nothing to export
To send out of London Port
Our trades are left in decimation.
Our skills are lost to this proud nation.

So progress is it?
Does anyone care? No not a jot?
Will we wake up and find it's too late?

BOBBY'S STORY

Ivy Brown

Bobby was a dear little puppy, but he could be very naughty. He used to chase cats in the garden and whenever he was taken to the park, would scare boys and girls by yapping and jumping at them. He even tried to steal their sweets and small toys.

"I don't think you would bully other children like that, would you?"

Bobby didn't mean to be nasty. He did it to get attention because he was bored and lonely. The lady who owned him loved him dearly, but she was quite old and not able to play with him. He did enjoy it though when she wagged a finger at him and told him to be good.

One day the front door was left open and he went for a walk. Unfortunately he lost himself. His owner was very upset when he didn't return home and realised that she could no longer look after a pet.

But everything turned out well, because the lady who found him knew a lot about dogs and it was agreed that she should take him into her care and give him special training.

Bobby is no longer a puppy and never misbehaves. He now works as a guide dog to a blind man. They are very happy.

My message to all children is, "Never feel bored - be nice to your classmates and you won't be lonely - work hard at your lessons and who knows - you may get special training and become very famous".

THE POPPY SELLER

Lewis Button

Give us a pound for a poppy mate,
For the men that saved your fate.
They never questioned what or why
Would we live or would we die.
How did I lose my legs, I'll tell you, sure?
It was at the fall of Singapore.
Three years I spent in Changi Jail
To break our spirits they're sure to fail.
But that's enough of me
You know it all it's history.

Today we're here to remember them
Who did not come back home again.
Standing in this sacred square
Nobility stands to praise us there
On the third side our head of state
Her head bowed down to contemplate.
Her brave subjects whose valour saved
Her sacred Kingdom, right to the grave

When all of the glorious and good have gone
The forgotten heroes march as one.
In such formation proudly march
Walking past, Admiralty Arch.
No longer with a soldier's stride.
Their bravery no one dare deride
Brave souls in wheelchairs ride
Who dares doubt a nation's pride
Their heads held high their eyes so proud
To the salute of the silent crowd.
The mothers, widows and children cry
And we who loved them wonder why.

It's a tale so old but still so true
Can I repeat it just for you?
When you question where or why
Wars are made by old men for young men to die

SKELETONS OF THE MIND

Jim Burns

Looking through the railings of my tenement block, the year 1938, seven years old, the place Alberta House, Poplar E14, poverty rife, but I might get a pair of new shoes.

Down below from the railings of the tenement block they were building an air raid shelter, thirty feet by fifteen feet, solid concrete and brick.

But across the River Thames the Docks were looming, the Thames full of ships. My Dad was working over time. He was a stevadore and he was loading scrap iron for German re-armament and I might get my first pair of new shoes.

There were nine in my family, eight brothers, one sister. All in three bedrooms, a main room for eating, a scullery, bathroom and toilet built by the LCC (London County Council), all different from where we came from which was a slum in an Irish ghetto, Rook Street, Poplar all in two rooms upstairs, downstairs a brothel.

Then like a bolt from the blue, I was lining up in the school playground with a gas mask box, a label on my collar and a bag of clothes. War had been declared and I was on a journey by train to who knew where.

Paddington Station packed with children, Mums, teachers, social workers, all organising the thousands leaving London in 1939.

This was an adventure I thought, green fields, cows, rabbits, buses, trains then Oxford Station.

Then the auctioneers took over. "I want a boy about 12 years". I looked up at the rafters of this old village hall in Wytham, near Oxford, bats flying, my elder brother and sister all up for auction. The fat man said to my eldest brother Bob, "It's going to be alright," as he guided us up a dark lane. We are going to the Abbey. "Oh no we are not" shouted Bob. me, my other brothers Charlie and Frank all crying. My sister Eileen had gone to a farmer.

60

Passing heavy wrought-iron gates, we entered the Abbey, maids in maroon dresses and white aprons made us welcome.

The next five years turned the four brothers into little Lord Fauntleroys. Gone were the slums and poverty of Poplar E14. Maids, butler, housekeeper, it was still upstairs and downstairs, but we had a wonderful time. Then like a bolt from the blue, the last all-clear had sounded, the war was over. I remember being bundled into a taxi back to Oxford Station, seeing the green fields and the cows and rabbits, lost in the dirt and smog as we arrived at Paddington Station.

I was now thirteen years old and aware of what I had lost, 'Paradise', the tranquility of country life, living in the wealthy Wytham Abbey.

Climbing the concrete staircase of the tenement, dark, the smell of urine mixed with the smell of the River Thames when the tide was out, the sound of fog horns floating over silent waters. I was back to poverty of bombed out London, the same greasy string that held the key in the letter box, the same greasy string that I had left five years earlier.

How I was going to survive haunted me for years, till at the age of eighteen years a brown envelope told me I was to do two years' National Service, either Malaya, Korea or Egypt, another frightening prospect of my life. The skeleton bones still rattle today, that same greasy string.

A TRUE FRIEND (A PET DOG)

Lewis Button

We've been good companions thro' these many years,

I've seen your eyes with laughter and seen you shed some tears.

You tended me and loved me like your child,

And how I rushed to greet, you just a-running wild.

There's one more thing to do for me I know will cause you pain.

Please let me go with love, don't let me ask in vain.

I can hardly bear to leave you, I love you all so much

So often did you stroke me I loved your gentle touch.

Remember me with kindness, think of me, don't grieve.

I'll stay within your memory that I'll never leave.

For were we not the best of friends

For true love and friendship never ends.

MY SON

Lewis Button

His dancing eyes his curly hair
I still see him standing there, my son
I still see his lovely smile
All the girls he would beguile, my son
His little joke, the way he spoke
How he mixed with all the folk, my son.

I cannot tell you how I miss
When home from work that little kiss, my son
Then he told he'd go to war,
As his father did before, my son
As the tears began to flow

I hid them well, he's not to know. My son

Then one day the letter I'd dread,
'Just to say he's reported dead, your son
He was I'm told so very brave,
His comrades he had tried to save, your son'

I must face each passing day
Without you, to light my way, my son
Like so many who went before
Dying on a foreign shore, my son

His father and I say not a word
Life wasted how absurd, our son.
Still you live in our mind
Your thoughts your deeds so very kind
The tears just flood make my eyes blind, my son

The military funeral cold as can be
Did not include your dad and me
The volley shot into the air
Just added more to our despair
For all we knew you weren't there, my son

STAIRWAY TO HEAVEN

Marion Osborn

"You must lock me up!"

Another nutter the sergeant thought. The third one he'd had to deal with tonight. Why did they all come in on his shift?

"I can't do that love. You've done nothing wrong", he replied patiently.

"But I'm afraid that I will. Please, please help me. Put me in a cell for the night so as I can't harm anyone".

She certainly looked strange the policeman thought as he stared at her more closely.

"I can't lock you up for something you **might** do".

The cells would be full to overflowing if I locked up everyone who wanted a bed for the night, he thought.

She grabbed his arm urgently.

"It's my voices. They tell me to do bad things and I'm afraid I might do something evil".

"Now, now dear. Best thing you can do is to go home and have a nice warm drink and go to bed. Do you know it's midnight and way past your bedtime" he said in his best avuncular manner.

He went round his desk and led her protesting to the door and eased her gently through. The woman walked off and he went back in shaking his head at the pity of it all.

Tears streamed down the woman's face unchecked. Nobody understood her torment. Whilst her mind was relatively lucid and at best she had tried this last throw of the dice to rid herself of her sense of impending doom. Since she had been released from the asylum she had battled against her demons. When they descended and clouded her mind the agony was dreadful. Why had they sent her away from the safety of the institution? Care in the community they called it. What kind of joke was that? She stumbled on. Then they started. Whispering at first.

"Kill. Kill. Kill".

Then gathering momentum, they got louder.

"KILL. KILL. KILL".

She rubbed her ears frantically, but it made no difference. You can't escape from your own head. She started running helter-skelter until she finally stopped, winded, gasping for breath outside a bungalow, which was in darkness. It was then that she heard a baby wailing. And the voices stopped!

Inside the bungalow Jennie awoke. Chloe was crying. She sat up sleepily and felt with her feet for her slippers. Beside her, Jeff stirred.

"Where are you going?" his voice was muffled with sleep.

"To see what's wrong with the baby".

"I thought we agreed to let her cry."

"She sounds upset. I'll just see if she's alright."

"What time is it? Don't tell me. It's 2 o'clock." He was wide awake now.

"Yes, but....".

"She's like clockwork. She's never going to let us have any rest while you keep going in to her. I haven't had a good night's rest for ages".

"I know you're right, but just let me go in this one last time..."

"You always say that. Look, just give it another 10 minutes - all right 5 then. Just to see if she'll drop off."

Reluctantly Jennie lay back on her pillow, mentally counting the minutes, listening to her baby's cries.

In the nursery, the woman was looking down into the cot. She had climbed in easily through the open window. It was a hot night and Jennie had left it open to give Chloe fresh air.

Jennie could stand no more. Every cry was like a dagger in her heart. She got out of bed. The crying suddenly stopped.

"There what did I tell you? Now perhaps we can get some sleep." Jason was triumphant.

Jennie got back into bed.

In the child's bedroom the woman was rocking Chloe in her arms. The feel of the comforting warmth of the woman's body had instantly checked her tears. The woman wrapped one of the blankets around the baby and stepped out of the window into the street.

She peeked at the baby. She was sound asleep. She walked on until she came to a stream and sat down on the grassy verge.

Then the voices started again.

"Drown her. Drown her. Drown her."

"No. No". She shook her head.

The voices got louder and louder until they built up to a crescendo.

"DROWN HER. DROWN HER".

Like someone in a trance she walked to the water's edge and laid the child in the water. The shock of its coldness awakened the child and she started struggling. The woman held her under and pressed her body firmly down until all movement stopped. Then she let her go and watched as the body floated away down stream.

The voices had stopped. Peace, perfect peace. That child would never know the agony she had known. She must get home. She began to hum "Stairway to heaven" gently to herself. She'd already eliminated what had just happened from her mind. Tomorrow was her birthday and she would be Queen of the May.

PURPLE

Marion Osborn

Purple is royal
Purple is rich
Purple is pomp
It's crown and its state

Purple is range.
Purple is bruised
Purple is passion
It's love and it's hate

Purple is plumage
Purple is velvet
Purple lines coffins
It's life and it's fate

THE VISITATION

Marion Osborn

Jade's eyes flicked open and fixed on a small child sitting on her bedside chair.

"Lois"? She uttered unbelievingly.

Then in the same second she realised it was not her daughter and her heart felt leaden again. Would the pain never end of losing her only child under the wheels of a speeding car exactly a year ago? Jade had come away for this holiday abroad alone, for as a single mother she had no partner to share her grief and no friend or relative could give her solace, because they could not empathise only sympathise and that was not enough. No never enough!

But had this child come with a message? For she knew instinctively she was a visitation. There was an eerie light emanating from her and the apartment that had been so stiflingly hot was now as cold as the grave. Besides she'd carefully locked the door before going to bed that night.

"Do you know Lois"? she asked.

The child looked at her with unblinking eyes and the saddest expression she had ever seen. Without answering she stood up and drifted to the door, then turned and beckoned to Jade, who got out of bed and although in her pyjamas, felt no compunction but to follow her outside.

Leaving the holiday complex she trailed the child at a distance. Then Jade realised that they were coming to the country lane which was lined with large private properties guarded by vicious guard dogs, which was completely taboo to her as she had a phobia about dogs. So she stopped terrified, her heart pounding with fear and sweat breaking out on her forehead and her feet

Jade moved as if in a dream past the houses, with the snarling dogs hurling themselves at the fences trying to get at her with their flashing teeth bared and their incessant barking deafening. Suddenly one broke through and leapt at her. Sinking to the ground she knew her last moment had come. Had this all been a trick for her to face her worst nightmare come true she wondered? She could smell the dog's fetid breath on her face, but before it could sink its teeth into her it ran off yelping to where it had come from. She opened her eyes. The child was at her side and sensing her ghostly presence must have frightened the dog. No longer afraid, Jade followed her through olive groves until they came to an old church. They stopped by a huge ancient olive tree, where the child indicated that she should dig.

"With my bare hands?" Jade questioned.

The child nodded. Buried shallowly was a small skeleton. She recoiled in horror, looking at the child, whose face had a most beatific smile spreading across it, illuminating her eyes, so that she noticed for the first time a line running down from one of her pupils like a big black tear drop.

<u>WORRY</u>

Marion Osborn

Worry that insidious creep
That pervades my brain until I cannot sleep.
Wide awake tossing and turning
Keeping the midnight oil burning

But still I cannot sleep.

When a glint of light through the mud does peep
Sour reason to the ground does **dash**
It's momentary **flash** of hope
And of little use is any form of dope

Once I am enveloped in it's crushing fold.

And still I cannot sleep
Yet everything passes so I am told
And even worry releases its tight hold
And so at last my mind cajoled
I gently snore and am asleep once more

A MOVING EXPERIENCE

Marion Osborn

I got on my bike and rode aimlessly around the streets.

My mum had said it would be a wonderful new life for us all. Away from the slums of London. A garden where we could play. A bedroom of our own instead of sharing my parent's room. A bathroom instead of the communal bath once a week and the Friday night ritual of the tin bath in front of the fire and the last one getting the coldest and dirtiest water.

Not that I cared about those things!

I missed playing in the street with the other children and the people and the friendliness. Everyone knowing everybody else and nobody better than anyone else.

Going down Charlie's second hand shop in Mornington Crescent on Saturdays and spending all your pocket money on a lot of old tat. Playing mar- bles on the manhole covers, the huge bonfire in the street with all the big boys jumping over it as the flames got higher and higher. The shrieks at their daring as they narrowly escaped getting their trousers burnt.

Dodging the jumping crackers and the lovely smell of chestnuts roasting, the thrill of staying up till after dark and the fun of it all. The lovely warm feeling of community and belonging. My heart seemed to swell until I couldn't bear it any more.

How I hated the new town with the endless streets and houses all looking exactly the same!

No landmarks at all.

My loathing intensified and my unhappiness was compounded. The ache of my longing for home was so physical that I felt numb with misery. Oh if only we could go back! But young as I was I knew we never could and that I would be happy again and then despised myself for my disloyalty.

There was no way that I could let my mother know how I felt because she had tried so long and hard to achieve the move.

But her joy moved me not at all.

I could only comprehend my own overwhelming homesickness as I came back full circle to the un-welcoming house that I hated with every fibre of my being,.

I pulled the key on the string through the letter box and let myself in.

"Is tea ready, Mum?" and my voice was cheerful.

REQUIEM FOR A RAW RECRUIT

Marion Osborn

The Wren Officer entered the room, glanced dispassionately at the figure of the young recruit and then picked up the letter, which was lying beside her.

Opening it she read:

Dear Mum

You remember how happy I was to get into the WRNS? How I said it was the best 18th birthday present ever? The newspaper placards outside the station that day, with 'Princess Grace gives birth to a daughter' plastered all over them? S'funny the things that stick in your mind, isn't it? But the day itself, all the tests I had to take, are like a blur to me now.

But Mum, it didn't turn out like I expected at all. I can tell you the truth now, but I couldn't before, in case it got anyone into trouble. You do see, don't you Mum?

I suppose it was all my own fault really - **allowing** it to happen. The bullying I mean. Alison Pike - I can say her name now - picked on me from the start. I didn't seem able to stand up for myself at all. I know we thought that going into the WRNS would be the making of me, help get rid of my beastly shyness for one thing - but it didn't.

She sabotaged everything I did, so that I was always in trouble, even to taking parts of my uniform so that I got put on charge for being improperly dressed on parade. Not only that, she turned all the other girls against me, so that no one spoke to me. And so it went on. I was so unhappy!

Then a new recruit came and she started on her. She had a field day with her because she was even softer than me, but she left me in peace. It was lovely! I did feel sorry for the new girl though. Her name was Celia - I say **was** - she committed suicide. Of course, it was all hushed up, But then she started on me again and it was worse than before.

I **did** stand up for myself one day Mum and asked her why she hated me so much - I admit I was crying when I said it. And d'you know what she did? She hit me so hard round the face that my ears rang, called me "pathetic" and walked off.

I can't see any way out Mum! That's why I'm doing this dreadful thing. They say that putting the gun in your mouth is the quickest and most painless way. I'm so **frightened** Mum, but if you show this letter to the CO it might stop anyone else from being bullied.

I do love you Mum, but I can't put up with it any longer. Please forgive me.

Love Jess

Alison smiled as she finished the letter, walked over to the fire and threw it into the flames and watched it burn to a cinder. She then left the room to report her grisly discovery.

THE ABBEY REVISITED

Jim Burns

The return of Mrs De Winters to the gates of Manderlay unfolded a drama which contained all the expected ingredients of love, hate, jealousy and murder. This story has nothing to do with that drama except perhaps the gates.

Situated on the outskirts of Oxford and built in Norman times, Wytham Abbey has played host to a motley crowd of inhabitants over the centuries, not least of those being a group of evacuees from the east of London who came to the safety of the mansion away from the Blitz which reduced the city to rubble.
Forty years after the end of World War Two, three of these young people - now middle aged, agreed to journey to Oxford in order to relive some past memories although they were unsure as to the reception by the surviving members of the Ffennel family. Hazel Ffennel had died at the age of twenty nine in mysterious circumstances and the Londoners found her grave neglected and overgrown. They remembered what a source of worry she had been to her parents. She had been a kind caring person who would help any 'lame duck' and often served out hot soup to the 'down and outs' in London, much to the concern of Hope and Raymond who for all their wealth, had been unable to prevent her death. The three elderly people stood in awe outside the massive iron gates, each thinking should we intrude? The rusty padlock seemed to be saying keep out. Jim, Charlie and Eileen thought that they should leave well alone and go home. They stood close together staring, saddened at the sheer desolation of the once fine Abbey that had been their home for five years in the dark days of the war. They recalled the maids and other servants, the housekeeper and butler, who had all helped to create a happy atmosphere for the cockney evacuees.
Standing mesmerised, their thoughts wandered to the carefree

games played in the rambling corridors, a far cry from their life in a crowded tenement block in Poplar, E14.

An old three-wheeled wicker invalid carriage lay rusting and rotting under a magnolia tree which showered it with white waxen petals. As they looked, recollections flowed back and they remembered how the tragic drama was played out.

They could almost hear the screams as Hazel verged on a nervous breakdown all those years ago because of her life long friend Miss Bartlett, who had showered unstinting care on the sad woman, the only daughter of rich parents.

Suddenly their nostalgic thoughts were interrupted.

"What you be a wanting"?

They turned quickly to see a man with a face like a wizened crab apple. His outdated clothes were rumpled and stained as he stared at them with suspicion from under his bushy eyebrows.

"We came to see the Abbey, said Jim".

"You got no business in there" said the old man aggressively, "so be off".

He moved closer to stare at the three Londoners. "Ain't you Mr Cherry"? asked Charlie. "I be". There was a pause as he moved even closer. "I knows your faces"!

"We're the three evacuees that lived here during the war".

"Well I be buggered - so you are - I thought I recognised you". His face lit up and his smile revealed tobacco-stained teeth.

"Let's see, you be Charlie, you be Eileen and you be that little varmint James". He started to laugh, which set him coughing and he spent the next few minutes laughing and coughing in turn. Finally he paused and suggested wheezily "Come and meet the missus, we often talk about you".

They walked slowly through the village, the familiar places bringing back many memories. Suddenly Mr Cherry stopped. "You can't go in the Abbey"!

The three visitors were puzzled, but they merely shrugged. Soon they arrived at the cottage next to the bridge and followed Mr Cherry inside, being careful to bow their heads and avoid the heavy beams. They saw a grey-haired woman sitting at a table.

"Look who be 'ere Ann - it's the evacuees from the Abbey. Well I be blessed," and she quickly looked at the three faces now aged with time.

"After all this time! I don't believe it," and you are my Snowy May - my first love," said Jim. Ann threw her head back and laughed. "Well I never! Come, sit down and have tea."

They all sat round the table drinking many cups of tea and enjoying Ann's home made scones. There was plenty of chat and laughter of bygone days. The sun was going down and they were thinking that it was time to go when Charlie blurted out "Why can't we go to the Abbey?"

All went quiet. The old man indicated to Ann and they went into the kitchen. The three visitors could hear hushed voices before Ann returned, her face looked strained.

"It be like this, Bob my husband is the caretaker of the Abbey. He don't like the job but gets a wage from Oxford University and it helps out, but it's not doing his health any good. The Abbey is being pulled about to make flats for students, but there are restrictions on what can be done, covenants it's called - that's the truth why nobody can go in. She paused breathlessly.

Charlie asked insistently. "Please - we came all this way and I want to know" - he stopped short.

Ann looked anxiously at Bob, "let them have a look, nobody will know. They are going home tonight and they did live there for five years." As she spoke Ann's eyes were searching Charlie's anxious face. Eileen then spoke up. "Leave it Charlie, we don't want to put his job at risk."

"Damn it, you will see it," decided Bob as he strode across to a cupboard and returned with a chain of keys.

Their happy childhood memories were dashed as they turned through the gates and saw the now fallen walls, the crawling ivy, the broken leaded windows streaked with pigeons' droppings. Bob fumbled nervously with the keys then opened the massive oak doors. The stench of mildew of the dead hit the fresh air. The oak staircase still swept upwards, but the beautiful Renaissance tapestry was gone from the far wall, leaving it black and grey.

Crossing the flag stone-floor, their steps echoed with the spirits of the past. Up the rotting wooden staircase, round the corner into a dark corridor, the smell was unbearable.

The sound of flapping wings sent a chill of cold sweat on their foreheads. "Mind the pigeons shit, it's a bit dark here," warned Bob as he tried to lighten the tense atmosphere.

"Ah, here's the Masters Room". More keys clanged. The setting sun lit up the bare cold room before dipping finally over the horizon.

"The Ladys' room is through there," said Bob, jangling yet more keys. "You won't be able to get to the other side of the house, all the floor boards are up. "But what about Miss Hazels' room," cried Charlie.

"Miss Weigalls' room is through there, you know the one that went off her rocker." Keys rattled again. Yes, Jim knew well seeing Miss Weigalls walking in the garden dressed only in a night dress talking to phantom people, saying she was going to Paris, seeing her sitting up in bed tearing up toilet rolls along the perforated lines.

"Miss Barletts' room is along a bit further". Bob seemed more like a jailer than a caretaker.

The three Londoners were witnessing the end of an era, no opulence, no sign of wealth, just bare rooms and the smell of death?

"And this is Miss Hazels' room," Bob said quietly. He opened the door and they all went inside. Immediately, the visitors sensed that something was wrong.

Charlie paced the floor, shaking his head. Eileen and Jim looked out of the window. The magnolia trees were hidden from their sight by the overgrown bushes and the little gate where the ponies had come to see Hazel every morning was lying hidden in the tall grass.

"No, no, no - this is not Miss Hazels' room." Poor Charlie was hysterical.

Bob and Ann had left the room. Eileen and Jim attempted to calm Charlie.

"Perhaps we've got it wrong", Jim said hopefully.

"I don't care," shouted Charlie. "This is not Miss Hazels'" room. His raised voice caused Bob and his wife to come back into the room.

"Ok," said Bob, "I will show you her room, but I must tell you I will be breaking the covenant. It's been sealed since she died."

"Leave it out Charlie", said Jim in a panic.

Bob led the way back down the dark corridor, turning right then left, moving in a circle until they were back where they had started, but at a different angle. New plasterboard walls had completely altered the appearance.

They eventually reached a door, which had been disguised by the plaster. Keys rattled again and the door groaned and squealed as Bob pushed it open. He walked across in pitch darkness, the full length shutters open slightly. The smell of mildew was as heavy and thick as the cobwebs, some furniture covered in dust sheets.

"This is it", screamed Charlie, this is Miss Hazels' room.

Cobwebs that had lain undisturbed for years, now floated in the foetid air. Charlie was jumping up and down, the dust now overpowering.

"There's Miss Hazel! I can see her," he screamed. Bob decided that was enough. "That's enough of that old mumbo-jumbo", his voice in a panic. "Out you go" and slammed the shutters and hurried them out of the room, more rattling of keys, then down the oak stairs and out in the fresh evening air.

It was with mixed feelings and puzzlement that they said goodbye to the caretaker and his wife.

Maybe Charlie did see Hazel, his desire to be in her presence was so urgent and demanding it overtook his normal good sense of judgement. Who knows! It's up to the reader to make judgement.

LAMBOURNE END

Jim Burns

A phone call came from a friend who ran a youth club called 'The Basement' in Cable Street, Stepney E1.

He told me about a piece of land at Lambourne End about half a mile from the Camelot Public House. The land was about half an acre with a large hut on it.

It had been given to the families of Stepney by rich Philanthropists. 'They can have good fresh air and enjoy the countryside; and so gave it to them.

This had been a regular holiday for the youth of Stepney, but over the years, through neglect or shortage of funds, the hut was unusable. The roof was badly leaking which meant that in the event of bad weather they had no shelter, so the campsite was not being used to its full potential.

My friend went on to tell me that he had been studying the documents regarding the covenant of land, that in the event of the land and hut falling into disrepair or not being used as intended, it was to be sold and he has already had enquiries from developers.

He asked me if I could get a local roofing repair firm to do the work. I said I did know a friend of mine who would do it if you paid for the materials. He agreed. He gave me the phone number of the caretaker who would give me the keys.

I met Lumpy the roofer and explained the situation. He agreed and would do the work at the weekend. He said he had a roll of roofing felt. We got the keys and drove to the site - the grass was high, but the size of the hut gave us a shock, it was 40' x 20'. We finished the job, but it took ten rolls of felt.

My friend the Youth Leader was over the moon and invited me and my family to the camp site when it opened.

And so for many years the families of Stepney still enjoyed the countryside of Lambourne End.

THE ADVERT

Doreen Pickering

Jane had just inserted an advert in 'Loot'.

Myrtle picked up her copy of 'Loot'. She scanned the page. Oh how marvellous; Someone was advertising an old fashioned chest of drawers. She had her Mother's bookcase and bureau from the old home and this chest of drawers would hopefully fit really nicely in the far corner of her room. She immediately made an appointment to see the chest of drawers. She had quite a long bus ride before alighting at the bus stop near to the house she was to visit. It was a cheerful-looking room that she was led into and the lady of the house was a vivacious and easy-to-talk to person. She soon had a cup of tea and a plate of biscuits by her side. They talked of this and that and when Myrtle saw the chest of drawers, it was perfect for her little corner and would blend beautifully with her room at home. She paid the £20, saying she would arrange to have it picked up as soon as possible.

Myrtle waited at the bus stop opposite to catch her bus home. The bus came quite quickly. Myrtle sat in the back seat and started to think about her old home and how her Mother would have loved this chest of drawers. So many memories came flooding into her mind. Suddenly she realised she was her stop. She jumped up from the back seat and rushed to the platform, just in time to alight before the bus started again.

She was in such a hurry to cross the road and get home that she didn't see the lorry behind the bus. Suddenly there was a screech of brakes and someone shouted "Watch Out"! A crushing feeling to her body and then oblivion.

ROAD TO NOWHERE

Marion Osborn

Flames were issuing from the bonnet of Pink's car. Terrified, she steered it onto the hard shoulder. Before she could get out, the car exploded and she was blown sky high.

Then why was she still here? Reincarnated so soon, or was she a ghost? Or had she dreamt the explosion? No, the wreckage of her car was scattered all around her and no way could she have escaped completely unscathed. Whatever the explanation, ghost or human, she realised that she had to get away from the motorway and so she set off.

As she trudged along, thumbing a lift, she began to regret her bizarre appearance, for vehicle after vehicle whizzed past her, showing no inclination to stop. She had to admit that her dyed fuchsia hair set in the Mohican style could be off-putting. But then she was a singer in a rock band. There was also her heavy eye-make up with thick black stripes painted across her cheeks, a shocking pink tee-shirt at least three sizes too small for her, exposing her bare midriff, with rolls of fat bulging over her black leather micro mini-skirt and chains hanging from its waist band. Clumsy high length boots completed the ensemble. Chains rattling, she clumped along the road. Then it started to mizzle and before long it was bucketing down. She looked a sorry sight, with the black make-up running down her face, but still nobody stopped for her.

"Probably think I'm some kind of thug," she thought, feeling sorry for herself. She sat down on a grass verge and started to sob, for her appearance belied her nature and she was a gentle soul at heart and wanted her Mum.

A van drew up. The window wound down and to her relief she saw a woman's face. She had a pleasant round face with a kindly smile.

"Are you alright luv"? Her voice had a soft country burr.

Pink got up and went over to the vehicle.

"My car broke down back there and no one will help me and I don't know what to do", the words tumbled out.

"You poor thing. You're wet through. Get in, we'll give you a lift, won't we dear"?

The man who was driving nodded his assent. Gratefully Pink got in.

"There are some dusters in the back there to dry yourself off with." Pink rubbed her face vigorously with them and with all her make-up gone, looked like a little girl, all large eyed with a tremulous mouth. The driver's eyes gleamed at her in the interior rear mirror and she responded with a shy smile.

"We'll take you to our place," he said. "We've got a daughter your age and you can borrow something of hers while we dry off your wet things. You'll be able to phone your Mum too."

"You're so kind. My name's Pink, what's yours?"

"I'm Fred and this is my wife Rosemary."

SEASONS

John Rogers

The prospect of a winters frosty day
Creates such a longing for a balmy warm summers afternoon
Spring pretends to promise everything but
Marching winds and April showers will not let the
Lovely flowers bloom too soon
At last quietly comes May, with buttercups
Daisies and daffodils strewn along her path
The hawthorn, elder flower blossom in the hedges
And Mother Nature tempers winters severe wrath
Young and old alike avoid all necromancy
Indulging to the full in whatever takes their fancy
Summer fast approaches as the sun retreats to
Concentrate his golden rays to encourage the wealth of colour
While sustaining the lives of the newly born.

ALL IN THE MIND?

Beryl Risbridger

I let out an involuntary yell as there was a loud bang behind me. Don't be so stupid, I chided myself, it's only the wind slamming the door, the same door I had walked through so cockily minutes before. How had I got myself into this situation?

It was my best friend Sue who had challenged me to spend two hours alone in this building, which was supposed to be haunted. She had always been into the occult, reading Tarot cards and I had always taken the micky and saying how naive she was to swallow all this rubbish, not that she took any notice. Never one to turn down a dare, this was how I came to be here now.

It was almost pitch dark and I had to feel my way around. Again I chided myself because I hadn't made a recci in the daylight, but I suppose that would have been cheating.

Oh God, what's that, my heart missing a beat as a huge black shadow flitted across the darkness. Sanity returned when I realised it was only the trees outside moving across in the moonlight. Thank heavens for the moonlight as it came out from behind the clouds.

For a short time the place was lit up and I got my confidence back. It's all in the mind, I told myself. How long have I been in here, looking at my watch. Only 10 minutes, it feels like hours. It went dark again, damn those clouds, but I had had a few minutes to get my bearings a little, so keeping my arms outstretched, I began to move forward.

I knew that I was in the huge entrance hall of a very old building, with many doors off, which I had got a glimpse of when the moon lit up the room. Somewhere my friend had hidden a smallish item that I was to find to confirm that I had actually gone right into this area and not cowered by the entrance door. She really was showing her confidence in me!!

My heart started thumping again as I heard what sounded like a moan. My imagination was working overtime.

Pull yourself together, you've found a logical answer to everything. Although I'd never admit it, I couldn't wait to get out of this place, it really was giving me the willies.

Put your mind to finding what Sue's hidden and stop scaring yourself. It helped that the wind had blown itself out and eventually I found the little package.

Thank God there's only five minutes to go. I emerged, telling Sue and her friends that it had been a doddle and I was even more convinced that it was all a load of rubbish - but in my quiet moments, I wasn't quite so sure.

AGEISM
Ivy Brown

Whenever I think of age
I know I've reached the stage
When friends and neighbours suspect I will
Eventually start feeling ill
They're always asking "Are you okay?"
Probably expecting me to say
"No, I'm in lots of pain
I don't think I'll get well again,"
But I'm glad to say it's not true
I'm fit enough for the things I do
So why do people make a fuss
When I run to catch a bus?
And why do passengers compete
When it comes to offering me a seat?
Do I really look as though
It won't be long before I go
I want family and friends to know the worst
It's possible that they'll go first
I hope not because I'll be alone
And you can't be happy on your own

CONVERSATION ON A BUS

Maureen O'Sullivan

1st Elderly lady boards bus, spots an acquaintance already seated
(2nd Elderly lady) and sits next to her.

1st EL Oh, hello dear. Haven't seen yer for ages. How've yer bin?

2nd EL (Pause) Me 'usband died.

1st EL (Appearing shocked) Oh I didn't know. Oh Dear! (Slight pause)
Oh, never mind eh!

2nd EL What yer mean?

1st EL What do you mean, what do I mean?

2nd EL Well it's a funny thing ter say, innit? Never mind, when me
'usband's dead.

1st EL I didn't mean anyfink by it. It's just like when people say 'How are
yer' and yer say 'Fine' when yer not fine at all, but it's just somefink ter
say! I didn't mean anyfink by it!

2nd EL (Impatiently) Ok Ok, forget it. You always did used ter come out
wiv stupid fings.

1st EL Wot yer mean?

2nd EL Well remember that time we was shopping and I went into the
hardware shop wiv you for some batteries and you asked for Durex instead
of Duracell!

1st EL Can't remember that!

2nd EL Well I certainly can. I was never so embarrassed. An there was
that time when your daughter was buying stuff on Ebay and she asked you
to go into the jewellers and price an ornament in the winder. It was Caper
De Monty or somefink

1st EL So?

2nd EL And you asked the man the price of the Aster Spoomanty in the
winder - and he burst out laughing?

1st EL I never did!

2nd EL You did an all!

Pause

1st EL Anyway, where is he?

2nd EL Where's who?

1st EL Yer husband. Is he in Barkingside or the new one?

2nd EL No. (Slight pause) He's on the mantelpiece. Haven't made up me
mind yet what to do with the old bugger.

SLAP OF LEATHER

Marion Osborn

I heard her before I saw her. That sensual sound of leather bound thighs slapping against each other as she climbed the stairs of the bus. Even though I was near the back, my ultra sensitive hearing picked it up and I waited with interest for her to emerge. I inwardly gasped with admiration - think Kate Moss - only taller and still with the bloom of youth, and you have her. But it was her trousers I envied and yes wanted. They were black, ultra tight leather and simply gorgeous. They took me back to my youth when I'd coveted a pair with all my being. But I simply could never afford them on my bank clerk's wages, for after giving up half to my Mother for housekeeping and half of the rest going on fares to London and lunches, there wasn't much left to play with. Not that I was disgruntled, except for those trousers.
The girl on the bus was sashaying up the aisle with a much smaller boyfriend in tow. She went right past me and made for the back seat and sat down with a slap of leather.

How I loved those trousers!

Who knows I mused, my life might have been entirely different if I'd been able to get some, I might have been discovered! My dreams were abruptly brought back to the present. The girl had switched on her i-pod or whatever they call them now and loud music - if you can call it that - filled the bus. It was reggae, which might be ok in small doses, but isn't my cup of tea. Then she shouted at her boyfriend above the din.
"I've got to be at the court at 11am" with four expletives in between.
I glanced at my watch, it was already ten past eleven and the court was at least half an hour away. I didn't hear her boyfriend's reply as he spoke softly.
But her reply came loud and clear.

"Well, they'll just have to hold everything up till I get there."

Again he must have replied, for she shouted above the din, "I don't want to know what she thinks about it. I've got enough with facing three judges", this time with even more expletives. I noticed that everybody else on the bus was looking rigidly ahead. No way was anyone prepared to turn round and register disapproval or make eye contact.

But still I loved her trousers!

I wondered what she'd done to warrant a court appearance. Her voice came loud again.
"I told you. I'm not interested in what she thinks and I don't want to talk about it anymore" and with that she turned the music up full blast. I didn't think it could have gotten any louder, but it was.

But still I loved her trousers!

My ears were hurting and I looked out of the window. It was Romford and my stop. I felt like running off the bus, but got up slowly along with several others. As I went down the stairs, I flickered a quick glance at the girl. Her face was stony and strangely, she didn't look pretty to me anymore.

But I still loved her trousers!

I noted that a couple of the people going down the stairs with me didn't get off, but sat downstairs to continue their journeys. I knew now why people didn't like sitting upstairs and why they said they never ever sat in the back seat.
But I still loved her trousers!

A GLIMPSE INTO PRE WAR CHILDHOOD MEMORIES

Beryl Risbridger

For many years my parents and I spent our holiday in quiet, sedate Littlehampton, but in 1937 it was decided that we would go to Ramsgate with relatives and this proved to be one of the happiest holidays I can remember.

We stayed in a boarding house, big enough to accommodate ten of us. There was my Uncle Charlie, Aunti Lizzie and Cousins Doug and George, Auntie Alice, Uncle Will and Cousin Betty, plus we three.

Every morning before breakfast, my Dad and I would walk down to the harbour to see the fishing catch come in. Anyone who knows Ramsgate will know that there are a hundred plus steps up the side of the cliff face and we climbed up and down these at least four times a day as we were booked with full board, which apparently was the norm in those days.

Each morning our Dads made us a sand motorboat, which George and I loved to play in. My Dad taught us to swim and a few years later, when evacuated, my Cousin swam a mile down the Bristol Channel, but as for me, the length of the pool was normally my maximum! We used to go back to our digs for lunch and would hang our swimming costumes and wet towels out of the sash windows. Our Mums may have just paddled their feet occasionally, but that was as far as they would go! When the tide was out, we used to play cricket or rounders on the firm sand and other families used to join in.

After lunch we would go back to the beach, but Betty and Doug, who were quite a few years older than George and myself, went off for a walk on their own. We were given a handful of pennies to play on the machines in one of the amusement arcades along the Prom. We became quite adept at them, never losing all our pennies and then, having a spell of winning, we amused ourselves for hours. Probably our parents got rid of us for a while whilst they had a nap in the deckchairs.

Then it was up the cliff stairs again and back to the digs. A wash, change of clothes and down to dinner.

After dinner the three families did their own thing, but met up at the bandstand an hour or so later.

If the tide was right, we used to walk along the sand to Broadstairs. There were caves into the cliffs to explore and large rocks to climb over.

Then we would all meet up at the bandstand where Billy Merrin and his Band played and one of his singers became quite famous later on. Her name was Rita Williams. How I loved that time, people dancing and singing, something so different to my quiet home life.

My Auntie Alice was a rather severe person to look at, but she was the most fun person I'd ever known and she got us doing all sorts of things. My favourite was the ten of us doing the Palais Glide all the way home. It was magic to an eight year old.

The following year we were lucky enough to repeat this holiday again and another Uncle and his family joined us for a few days. I don't think we were old enough to realise the storm clouds starting in Europe, but there was a much more important thing happening much closer to home, because Auntie Alice went into hospital and sadly died at the much too early age of 49. She was adored by the whole family, young and old alike and has never been forgotten even to today. Her only daughter Betty sadly died a few years ago, aged 87 and was a very caring person herself, but George and I are now the only ones left.

These two holidays left me with lasting, happy memories of that time.

WINTER

Vera Downes

The last of the winter leaves have drifted down
Through a pale sunlight that lingers.
The earth lies awaiting the cold embrace

Of winters icy fingers.

The voices of the birds are hushed
And a deepening silence grows,
The cruel beauty of hoary frost
Upon the hedgerow glows.

We awake one morn to a world transformed
By crystal satin lace,
Gone is the rubble and chimney stacks,

White castles stand in their place.

Winter is not a dying time,
The end of everything;
It is a time when nature rests
To pave the way for spring.

PRECIOUS IS THAT MOMENT

Bartholomew John

That teardrop on the cheek of the infant
That raindrop in the heart of the rose
That dewdrop on the web of the spider
Rare moments. Nature will ever impose

That sun on your face in the morning
That breeze in the heat of the day
That glorious twinkle of starlight
Rare moments, which always will stay

That lusty cry of the newborn
That mating call of the wild
That song of the Thrush and Blackbird
Rare moments for every young child

That orchestra's swelling concerto
That soprano commanding that chord
That rhythm and music combining
Rare moments we have to applaud

That catch of the breath as eyes meet
That pounding of blood in the ears
That one tender kiss, so sweet
Rare moment allaying all fears

That memory everyone clings to
That one word we always regret
That angry scene so untrue
Rare moments we never forget

Thank God for each precious moment
Which has fashioned a lifetime for me
No reason on this Earth to lament
The acceptance of what is, is to be

SWAN VIEW

Bartholomew John

I have always liked fishing ever since the day my Father first let me play with a small fishing net. There is something of the cat and mouse in it. Essentially the one thing you learn is patience coupled with an acceptance of failure, which in time becomes one of the main lessons of life.

Many happy hours have I spent, on river banks and lake shores all over the place. Always alone. Resentful of intrusion and in harmony with nature in all its moods.

I find that even now with a brief glance at the morning sky I am aware of the temper of the water. Believe you me, water is indeed temperamental, depending on the luring of the clouds, direction of the winds and colour mood of the sky. It can be dour grey, serene blue or a sheet of beaten burnished bronze. Whatever the mood. To me it has always been a form of therapy no psychiatrist could ever understand or recommend.

My name is Patrick O'Brien, thirty eight years of age and since my dear wife passed away last year, very lonely.

A lot of my time is spent sitting for hours gazing with an inner accepted calm at my ever changing surroundings. I suppose communing with nature, perhaps that sounds egotistical, but the recent experiences on the last few years have made me realise how fortunate I have been.

A few years ago I took up fishing as a hobby. My wife used to accompany me and I like to think she got as much pleasure out of it as I did, we liked the solitude of each others company.

When she had gone I was at a loss and found solace in just sitting near a small hidden lake we had found together, it brought her back to me in a way, perhaps it was the silence. There are very few fish there. I think those that are there know me very well. I feel we have a mutual agreement. Now and again they used to let me catch a youngster, just to teach them how not to be caught by strangers, for they knew I would always put them back.

On a small island in the middle of the lake lived a pair of the most majestic and beautiful swans I have ever seen. I had known them for some years when my wife was with me, but they became so much more important to me afterwards.

The male cob was so big and powerful. We had named him Hercule Bianco and his beautiful dazzling white Penn Perfecta Bianco a dream in her own right and very conscious of her well preened beauty.

Over the years they had accepted us both and proved a great comfort to me in my solitude. I could talk my heart out to them and they kept my secrets.

Although I still took a rod and line as an excuse just to sit there it was only a subterfuge to hoodwink passers by, they sometimes asked "Caught anything mate?" when I replied "No" they would look at me in a pitying way.

Over the year my swans had raised many lovely cygnets, sons and daughters, teaching them to swim, to live and finally to fly away. That was always the sad time, until their courtship was renewed again and I was happy to witness the elegant protestations of fidelity which brought forth yet two more eggs to be hatched and guarded. They took turns night and day and I was always on tender hooks until they both hatched, even after that I used to worry and spent as much time as I could with them.

Earlier this year I was preparing for yet another lazy day with my friends. While shaving I heard the Radio Announcer say that a small plane from our local aerodrome was missing. I remember hoping to myself that the person in it was safe.

I was not prepared for the sight that met my eyes when I finally reached my lake, sure enough, there it was, a shocking monstrosity a flagrant intrusion into our privacy, with it's nose buried in the centre of the little island. It was obvious by the wealth of pristine white feathers floating on the water surface that Perfecta had been sitting on her eggs at the time. I could not contain my sobbing breaking heart as I realised that yet another wonderful experience of my life had been so cruelly ended.

Standing on part of the fuselage was Hercules, so sadly majestic, his proud white neck was to one side as if in submission to the inevitable and his eyes seemed fixed on a far horizon.

When he became aware of me he came nearer, his eyes were now on mine, knowing he was mute I was surprised to realise that thoughts were being formulated in my mind beyond my control.

"We came to respect you and your kind for we felt you loved us, we the lesser ones of your world believe in and practice the very same moral principles that you do yourselves, love hate, an eye for an eye a hurt for a hurt. I now have to leave this place we were so pleased to share with you for I have yet to fulfil my destiny. I will tell of you and maybe some day one of my people may return".

So saying with slow measured strokes of his wings, he took to the air and I watched through my tears as he too rapidly became but a dot in the distance.

I collected two lovely long white feathers from the pool, which are mine to grieve over.

I reported the accident, the local services were soon on the scene. They found the poor pilot still alive, though badly injured. It took a long long time to clear the wreckage away.

Now it has gone I find it easier to come and sit and remember for I know in my heart that one day there will be the slow swishing beat of wings and a white new image will settle in my little heaven and I will be there.

ROLL UP ALL THE FUN ON THE FAIR. OH WHAT A LOVELY WAR. AT SIXPENCE A GO

Jim Burns

Get in line
Don't rush
Plenty of time
It will still be there
When you get to the
End of the line!
Oh! What a lovely war.
At the end of the pier
All for sixpence a go
You will see it all before you.
Put your eye
To the telescope of life.
What is that over the mountains?
It's the Khyber Pass
And the rusty remains
Of Britain's lovely war
Or is it Russian remains
Of its lovely war,
Or is it American remains
Of its lovely war
Against the Taliban?
So the war lords
Can plant their lucrative
Poppy seeds
And the spectre of
Bin laden and al-Qa'eda
Oh! What a lovely war
Pay no need
There's no need
There's a lovely war
Next door
In Iraq.

Our one time friend Saddam
His statue came crashing down
Who gives a damn
For a mirage of weapons
Of mass destruction?
After a thousand years
Of the rack and a month of
Mass bombing,
We tell them you will have
Our democracy like it or not,
Don't walk away
You can have your say
But don't mention
Guantanamo Bay.
Oh! What a lovely war!
It makes the blood boil
When we know
It's all about oil.
Seen enough, well that's tough
There's still Palestine and Lebanon
And wait if you can
There's always Iran.

CHANCE ENCOUNTER

John Rogers

This club was new to me. I had been a member for perhaps three months and did not know many people very well. One day some years ago, I was sitting quietly on my own
enjoying a nice pint of beer. On a nearby table were a couple of other chaps deep in conversation, I did not know either of them. Suddenly one of them turned towards me and said "I know you, you are Rogers, the last time I saw you was on the landing beach at Pachino Sicily nearly fifty years ago".
I replied "I am afraid I don't know you mate".
"Change my white hair to ginger, now what do you think"?
"No I really don't know you"
"How does Lenny London appeal to you"?
"Blimey! That little stroppy bastard, always looking for a fight".
"Yeah and you were always the flash bastard forever showing off".
We entered into a tirade of some make believe and spurious reminiscences.
He had been a member of this club a lot longer than me. I found out that he was an Iron Fighter, or more mundanely a Scaffolding Erector. He seemed to like the name Iron Fighter. He certainly had not changed.
Our families met socially for a couple of years, then I believe Mrs London became ill.
Surprising what a chance encounter can develop into.

LOST LOVE

Vera Downes

An old man sits by a dying fire
Just gazing at the embers
His eyes are dim, his body frail
But still his mind remembers

The hopes and joys of yesterday,
The laughter and the tears
The worries and achievements
Now tarnished with the years

The friends he had met along life's way
Alas now all departed
And like a vision shines 'that face'
Which leaves him broken hearted

The house now waits so quiet and still
No more the dog will bark
The sun goes down and twilight comes
And soon it will be dark

ESSEX BEGUILED

John Rogers

Tear stains on the face of an infant
Raindrops in the heart of a rose
Dewdrops defying the spider's intent
Such moments will nature impose
Bright sun in the sky at daylight
Soft breeze in the heat of the day
Night ceiling of exquisite starlight
Such moments will not fade away
An orchestra's swelling concerto
A tenor commanding high notes
Enchanting, thrilling crescendo
A barefoot boy herding goats
The lusty first cry of the newborn
Fierce mating calls of the wild
Birds of song in the blackthorn
Each scene has Essex beguiled.

ESSEX IN THE EAST

John Rogers

Essex is my County home, though I have a high regard for
Devon.
Hainault is where I chose to live, one stone's throw from Heaven
Essex has few hills and dales, yet numerous country lanes.
Essex boasts of streams and brooks, rivers and grassy plains
Essex greets the sun at dawn, along marshes, sands and sea
Essex colours the whole wide world in majestic mystery.

WHAT HAPPENED TO MY HEAVEN

Bartholomew John

I were born to Fiddlers Hamlet, yonder by Epping way
Begotten in a frenzy, in a field of Hainault Hay
My Father was a Verderer who walked by now and then
I was told he took one look at me and was never seen again.

My Mother was a big buxom wench all of eighteen stone
Me poor little bugger was nought but skin and bone
I lived a life of freedom in and out those fields so green
Even more exciting were the bits of forest in between.

Proud Oaks, Silver Birch and twisted Hornbeams flourished there
I became an expert catching both the rabbit and the hare
The badgers lived on the hill we called Brocket Way
Intriguing the long rabbit mound named Burrow Road today.

The Arrowsmith fashioned my first bow and taught me how to shoot
The very first victim of the fletcher was a bald faced coot
I never killed for pleasure, no matter what I shot
We were poor enough and hungry much more often than not.

Farmer Manford had three fields verging on Romford Road.
One he fattened young bullocks in, the other two he sowed
One day all his stock escaped, it was nearly a total loss
Servicing every cow in sight with a new breed called Manford Cross.

So my growing years went by and I were happy as could be
Never dreaming what the future held in store for me
I were trapped I were, silly me, like a rabbit in a snare
No matter where I went, I only had to turn my head she was there.

She kept on and on, her grinning face fair got me in a muddle
I had rolled her in that Hainault Hay, just a tickle and a cuddle
All her blooming family were chasing me all over,
Different altogether had I done her in the Clover.

99

They all called to harass my old Mum, saying we should be wed
All her Father got for his pains was a piss pot over his head
They went away swearing and threatening to get even,
I had a right old punch up with her older Brother Stephen.

Things got very hot for me just as the War broke out
For Stephen had been murdered without a shadow of a doubt
He had been shot with a rifle bullet right in the back in the head
And I was the very first suspect the minute they found him dead.

They found the rifle the very next day, finger prints wiped clean
For the life of me I could not remember where on earth I'd been
I knew I had been to a party, got drunk but nothing further
In no time at all I was indited on a charge of murder.

The old lady took it very hard, she nearly went insane
I had reason enough and time enough, the evidence was plain
In No.1 Court at the Old Bailey, Police evidence seemed to falter
After some debate, they dropped the charge to manslaughter.

I will never forget that terrible day waiting for the finding
When they found me guilty, inside it was like a coil unwinding
I was sentenced then to fifteen years, no chance of leniency
No one will ever know what those long years did to me.

They let me out a month ago, with a suit and seventy pounds
I have not got over the shock, since I've done the rounds
My home has gone, I'm on my own, my relatives all are dead
Where our caravan had rested, they have built The Alfreds Head.

My fields are all little boxes, full of people, dogs and cats
Smelly cars and concrete roads interspersed with bloody flats
I have lived out here in Hainault since I was barely seven
Why, oh why, did this have to happen to my idea of heaven.

People have to live somewhere, I am quite aware of their pains
The only reason they took my fields was because of the bloody trains
There is a sequel to all this, wry jokes come no bigger
Before my old lady died, said it was she that pulled that trigger.

RETRIBUTION

Maureen O'Sullivan

I had a nightmare about spiders the other night. They were inside my quilt cover, sewn into the seams, their long, thin legs struggling to escape. Dozens of them. I woke up screaming. The next morning there was one in the laundry basket. A short furry legged black one. I particularly hate those! But I couldn't kill it. When I looked again, it was gone. Later on I saw it on the other side of the kitchen, in the corner by the back door. A long distance to travel, for a spider. Then, later still, it was near the hinge of the hall door. I could have shut the door and killed it, without having to touch it. But I could not kill it.

But I did kill my sister.

I cannot pretend her murder was not premeditated. Oh yes, I had thought long and hard about killing her. I had planned it, looked forward to it like a child to a birthday party. I had carefully weighed up the pros and cons, considered the consequences, thought very seriously about whether I had the right to put an end to her life and all in all I had come to the one conclusion. Yes!

Quite simply, she deserved to die! She had not harmed me physically, but she had destroyed my happiness, the spontaneity of my laughter, the serenity of my slumber, the joy in my soul. Yes, she deserved punishment - but could I really bring myself to kill her? Could I be her judge and executioner?

When I saw her again after so long the answer was there in her own eyes. Her evil eyes which transformed in front of me. Like something you might see in a film.- Dr Jekyll turning into Mr Hyde - but this was reality. What had I done to deserve such hatred?

And seeing the evil again cloud those eyes I felt no compunction in placing my hands, my usually weak, caring, women's hands, around her throat and squeezing, harder and harder, until her face turned purple, the veins in her neck bulged and the shutters came down, finally, closing those eyes for ever. She had hardly struggled. I let go of her and she fell to the floor at my feet. I stepped back. I felt no remorse, rather a sense of triumph. I was satisfied.

I remember sitting by her body until eventually someone came. I can't remember who it was. Then all hell seemed to break loose, with somebody crying, sirens screaming from a distance and, as they approached, blue lights danced around the walls. I remember police and paramedics racing into the room, grabbing me, working on her.

Hours later, it seemed, I was bundled into the back of a police car. I didn't ask to have my coat over my head. Then questions and more questions. Probing, always probing. At last, the peace of a cell and blessed sleep.

After that day time passed in a kind of haze. Days turned into weeks, weeks into months. Hours of interviews, by police, psychologists, psychiatrists, my defence team. I welcomed the time I spent alone, away from prying eyes.

My day in court finally arrived and eventually I found myself in yet another cell, awaiting the verdict. I'd said little in court, responded briefly to questions. I didn't want anyone's mercy. I'd pleaded guilty, which of course I was, but due to diminished responsibility, which I knew wasn't the case, but at least it placated my defence team.

I'd watched the jurors watching me. Some openly hostile, some curious, one or two almost kindly. I smiled at them. They turned away.

I'd sat for hours in the cell, awaiting their verdict. I felt very calm, very controlled.

I stretched out on the uncomfortable bench seat with its thin inadequate padding. I shut my eyes. When I opened them, the light of the winter's day was beginning to fade, although it was only 3.30. If they didn't reach a decision soon, it would be held over until after the weekend.

As I lay there in the dusk I noticed a spider's web above my head, near the high veiling. It was moving gently in a draught. A large, brown, long legged spider picked its way across the web. Its precision fascinated me. Surprisingly I wasn't scared. I'd had worse company of late, I thought. Mesmerized, I watched its progress. It began to lower itself on a silken thread turning gracefully round and round like a trapeze artist. I noticed that its head was a paler colour than the rest of its body. As it came nearer and my eyes focused more clearly in the dim light, I saw the spider's eyes, darkly familiar. Eyes which glowered at me with a strangely human expression. Evil eyes. Advancing towards me. It was then I heard the screaming - terrified, demented screaming, coming from somewhere, someone. The door crashed open and two wardens burst into the cell.

It was then that I realized the screams were mine.

MEALTIME MEMORIES

Beryl Risbridger

I have to go back to May 8th 1945, the day the War ended, to write about a memorable meal.

How this particular meal was arranged so speedily is still a mystery to me, but it did happen in almost every road in London.

From early morning trestle tables appeared from somewhere, red, white and blue flags and coloured lights were unearthed from some source and we young ones were given the task of putting them up everywhere possible. It was a lovely warm and sunny spring day. After the austere greyness of the past six years, it felt like something magical was happening.

I lived in a small road which finished at one end by the railway, so the previous night a piano had been dragged out, a bonfire had been lit and many of us had very little sleep that night, but who cared!!

The tables were set up in a long line, white tablecloths put on them and chairs set each side. The tea party was basically to be for the young children and for such a small road there were a surprisingly number of them. There were very few men around as most of them were away in the Forces.

Over the morning tins of food we hadn't seen for such a long, long time appeared from nowhere. The unsung heroes of the War, our Mums, had managed out of our quite meagre rations, to somehow provide a feast fit for a king. Even a Box Brownie camera, complete with a film and I still have on e of those photos of me standing behind those excited young children seated round the tables, who probably had no real understanding of what was happening, but enjoyed it all.

I happened to glance to my right and couldn't believe my eyes, for there was my Dad striding down the road in his uniform, having bunked home from his RAF Station, risking 'Jankers' just to be with my Mum and me. Although only 15 years old then, the depth of emotion I felt at that moment, with the realisation that my family had survived, has stayed with me for the rest of my life. I only have to close my eyes and I can visualise and feel everything of that day, so I can genuinely say it was the most memorable meal of my whole life.

THE PANTOMIME

Lewis Button with special needs children

The excitement grows with every minute,
Children gasp at who is in it.
Noisily they scamper to their seats
With twisted legs and a bag of sweets
The music starts the kids all shout
The tension rises as lights go out.
The most wonderful sound you'll ever hear
Are children laughing and children cheer.
No time now for all their woes
They're going to see the king of shows.
Faces shine with expectancy
Transferred into worlds of infancy.
In wheelchairs they sit with eyes aglow
In a wondrous tale when lights are low.
The evil witch gets booed and whistles
As on the stage she glowers and bristles.
Then Jack's about to slay the giant
We all love Jack he's so reliant
Then take me to the toilet Miss
But hurry please we'll miss the kiss,
That Jacks about to give his girl
Jill's her name such a sweet pearl.
He saved her from the wicked Ogre
Before you know it is all over.
Back to school to tell their Mothers
And the sister and their brothers.
They'll find it hard to sleep tonight,
The day was filled with such delight.
So bye bye kids see you again next year
Whilst I just shed a silent tear.

HAUNTED?

Ivy Brown

When Katie sat down to breakfast her mother, Sue, noticed how quiet she was.

"Is there something wrong"? she asked.

After some hesitation the girl replied

"I didn't know Gran was a ghost".

"What are you talking about"?

"She came to my room in the night and told me to pay more attention to my schoolwork because you and Dad will be upset if I don't pass my exams. It was really scary."

"It was just a dream. You must be feeling guilty about wasting time instead of studying properly."

"No, it was definitely a ghost."

"Don't be silly ", said Sue, firmly. "You were close to your Gran, it's only natural you should dream about her sometimes. Now hurry up or you'll be late for school. Don't tell the other girls you've seen a ghost because they'll make fun of you".

As Katie left the room and made for the front door her father came downstairs.

"Hello darling", he said "Mind how you go. I'll see you tomorrow. I won't be home tonight - I have a late business meeting in town. Bye!"

"What's up"? Barry asked his wife. "Why were you angry with Katie"?

"She's up to her tricks again. It's all part of the scheme to get me to agree with you about moving house. First she moaned about her room being too small, then she kept complaining about quarrelling and dog barking coming from next door during the night. She'd do anything to get away from that school - she hates it. Did you put her up to all this"?

"Of course not! Although I still can't see why you won't agree to move. I need to be nearer my job and the house is in need of repair".

"This was my parent's house and I am satisfied with it. We are not moving."

With that Barry left for work.

That night Sue was awakened by tapping noises and groaning. Where was that coming from? She tried to switch on the bedside lamp but it wouldn't work. Just then a figure glided across the room and out of the door. She couldn't see who it resembled, the head was well covered. Was she dreaming? Then she heard giggling.

"Katie!" she mumbled, "I'll kill her."

Jumping out of bed she went to her daughter's room. But the girl was fast asleep. She checked the rest of the house, but found nothing out of the ordinary. Nothing seemed to be missing so it couldn't have been a burglar.

By this time she was shaking and couldn't bring herself to go back to bed. Were they being haunted?

In the morning she asked Katie if she'd heard anything unusual during the night.

"No Mum. I slept all night - making up for what I missed the night before. Are you ill? You look very pale."

"I'll be alright. Off you go to school."

On the way Katie phoned her cousin David.

"Hello Dave, it's me. You did a terrific job last night. I think it worked. Mum thought it was me, but I pretended to be asleep. Did you get home without your Mum finding out?"

"Yes" he said, "But I didn't think I was going to make it out of your house before your Mum caught me."

After dinner that evening, when Katie had gone upstairs to do her homework, Sue took hold of Barry's hand.

"I've been thinking things over" she said, "You are right about the house being in need of repair. I am willing to move after all."

"That's great!" Barry smiled. "But you must realise your relatives and friends will try to persuade you to change your mind again."

"Don't worry, dear" she replied. "They don't have a ghost of a chance."

THE MARRIAGE OF JOHN N' FLO
J G Dyer

John Thomas and Flo were to marry, quite soon they were going to wed

She'd bought a new dress, him a new suit, Banns at the church had been read

Flo thought she'd got what she wanted, John Thomas nuptual bliss

That's all he'd had his whole mind on, but Florence would have none of this

Her mother said "Look here our Florence, what about transport to church"

"We don't want to be left here stood standing or you to be left in the lurch"

Said Florence "We'll hire a roller or two, not those things I put in my hair"

John Thomas stood there awe struck "Hold on there" he yelled "I declare"

"Rolls Royce's I say are expensive, they don't run to churches for free

And this talk of renting a roller or two you're really not thinking of me"

Mum butted in she should not have done "How about tandems" she smirked

Flo yelled "Oh yes, with oil on my dress John Thomas you're really a burke"

"To hell with all this sarcasm" Quoth John "Just try to meet me half way"

The mother just stood there quite silent and Florence not one word to say

"I'll give you a start" said John Thomas sarcasticly "I'll hire a horse and a cart

Flo can ride like a queen, but I won't be seen I've just had a big change of heart.

COMMUTING TO GLOUCESTERSHIRE

Vera Downes

Fast cars and motorways
Prime essential speed
Every road is similar
No matter where they lead

Hours and days of boredom
As we swallow up the miles
Caged in gloss and leather
Just sitting getting piles

Zooming through the countryside
So dashing and so bold
Always new frustrations
And quickly growing old

As the tarmac slips away
So do hopes and dreams
Which vanish like the morning mist
And nothing's as it seems

H.F.C.A. (How Far Can Anyone)?

John Rogers

There is a place in Hainault where I never feel ill at ease
Where friends and strangers will always pass the time of day
Management and staff do their best to please
No reasonable request is ever turned away

There is such a lot of interest, many things going on
Like a little cosmic World of it's very own
Taking part in any of it one is never put upon
And it is very rare to hear a moan or groan

It is indeed foremost a wholesome family club
With activities catering all the time for all
The atmosphere is like an English country pub
Subject to the happenings in the entertainment hall

One can celebrate the wedding and the birth of the first Child
Enjoying such occasions with relations and friends
Such happy occasions never seem to get too wild
Yet most are reluctant to leave when the party ends

There is a myriad of happenings as time goes by
Wrestling with the ever present fat in keeping fit
Chin in, chest out, keep those legs up high
They flog themselves to death, save feeling such a twit

Pensioners enjoy a wealth of well considered care
Bingo and the chance to put the whole world right
Old fashioned passions are inflamed while there
They soon subside with the onset of the night.

There is always a driving force in such a successful community
Here the committee and its leader must take all the blame
How can they expect to enjoy a blameless immunity?
When every member can point a finger and name a name

WOW!

Ivy Brown

As soon as I saw him
My heart missed a beat
He was the handsomest man
I ever did meet

He looked into my eyes
And gave me a smile
I hadn't been so excited
In quite a long while

I realised I adored him
It didn't take long
But he couldn't have felt the same

For in no time he was gone

For days I was unhappy
Why did I let him go
Would we ever meet again
I really had to know

In fact I saw him many times
But to no avail, because
As I expect you've guessed by now
He's the man who never was

There is no one quite so perfect
In real life - so it seems
As he who appears before me
Only in my dreams

A MEMORABLE TEACHER

Maureen O'Sullivan

The most memorable teacher I ever knew never actually taught me. At least not in a classroom. He was my father.

He left school at a very early age. He had been awarded a scholarship to the London College of Architecture, such a momentous event in those pre-War days that the whole of his school was awarded a day off. However, despite the pleadings of his head teacher and class teacher, his mother refused to allow him to take up the scholarship, insisting that he start work straight away; something he never forgave her for. So he began working in a wood yard in East London, until the War came along and he joined the Army.

My father had always been a compulsive reader and throughout the War years he never stopped studying. Then when the War ended, by which time he was married with a small child, he was accepted by a teachers' training college in Folkestone. The following years were hard for my mother, with a second and then third child, my father away from home during his training period and even once employed as a teacher, money was very scarce. She had emigrated from Ireland when only 16, so had no family to support her and it is bizarre that although we were probably the only professional family in our road, we were also possibly the poorest!

My father started teaching in Poplar in East London in the late 1940's, a school lucky to be still standing among the debris of War, where children played in derelict houses and rubble strewn gardens. Many of them were without fathers, or with traumatised or damaged fathers, new fathers, or even a succession of fathers. Some of them had seen members of their families and neighbours killed. School was often their only stability in a world turned upside down.

It was only many years later, when I was an adult, that I realised how highly regarded my father was as a teacher. Not just by his colleagues, but by the many hundreds of children who had passed through his hands. Over the years he frequently received letters of thanks from pupils and their parents, for support given, exams passed, ambitions achieved. In retirement he continued teaching very successfully, tutoring children who were either struggling to fulfil their potential in sometimes crowded classrooms or suffering from a succession of experimental Government initiatives.

In the year my father turned 84, thanks to 'Friends Reunited', he received an e-mail from a past pupil inviting him to a re-union dinner in London with other former pupils who were celebrating their 60th birthdays that year. As they had moved to secondary school at the age of 10, it had been 50 years since they had met my father. He was the only one of their teachers they had managed to find still living.

I accompanied my father to the dinner at a very plush West End hotel. The re-union was attended by abut 30 former pupils and their partners. Many had travelled from far away, New Zealand, the United States and various parts of England. This was quite an experience because not only did they remember my father with great fondness and very high regard, but he remembered them all, not just by name, but their skills and talents, the sports some of them had excelled in, their siblings, their families etc. He mentioned them all by name in his after dinner speech. He spoke for almost half an hour with no notes, no hesitation. To say his audience were impressed is an understatement. Surprisingly, for people who had not had the most secure of childhoods, due mainly to the War and its aftermath, they had all done exceptionally well in life, most of them were professionals, some owned their own businesses, all very successful and every one of them said how much they owed to my father. What a inspirational teacher he had been. How he had enthralled them, opened up the world of literature, even of classical music, to them. How he had encouraged them and given them confidence and self esteem. The plaudits went on all evening. The night had turned from being a re-union to a tribute.

My father had always waxed lyrical about his teaching years in the East End. Like most families, I suppose it had very much gone in one ear and out of the other but that night I heard it from the horses' mouths! I could not have been more proud.

Another re-union was to be organised in 2009 to celebrate the year of their 65th birthdays. Unfortunately my father died last summer at his retirement home in Ireland. I know he will be with them in spirit.

(1935) OFF TO THE GOOD LIFE

J G Dyer

Before he left school at fourteen, Geordie had jobs helping the coal merchant, the petrol deliverer and others, anything for a couple of pennies. The tanker driver John Davis in particular was to play a big part in his life inasmuch that he would be the first person to help him on the quest of fulfilment. It happened that the railway lines with the goods yard were at the bottom of our street, almost forming part of it, with petrol wagons being shunted in on a twice weekly basis. Petrol was not sold as it is today, but on garage forecourts, even though it was only three pence a gallon and why Buck, (as he was always known), got into the habit of assisting John in the evenings, loading his tanker wagon with petrol from the railway wagon and the sealed cans from the underground store, ready for the next days delivery. He would often take Buck to his house where his wife would give him a welcome meal, plus he would get a couple of coppers at the weekend. Things were different now, he had left school and needed a proper job of work, for several weeks he had searched but to no avail, there was no work and the number of dole men standing idly at the railway crossing gates was growing. The thought of spending his life with them was daunting to say the least. His sister was in 'service' in London which put the idea into his head to go there, her recent letters bore little encouragement of this, but anything was worth a try. Bucks mind was finally made up when John Davis told him he was going on a long trip to Coventry to pick up a new tanker wagon early Saturday morning. After warning Buck of the pitfalls which should really have come from his father, he offered to take him to Coventry and help him on his way to London.

Saturday morning, at six o'clock, Buck wrapped up a couple of sandwiches, then leaving a note for his father, set off through Newcastle then on to the great north road. Tankers could only travel at a low fixed MPH so it was hours before they made their first stop with a flask of tea and a corned beef sandwich. (Buck kept his jam sandwich for later). At long last, when they reached the depot to get his new tanker, John bought dinners in the works canteen before looking around. At last he found what he had been seeking and led George across to an older man called Tom, explaining the situation.

Turning to Buck, he said Tom would take him near to the 'smoke' as he called it and help him. John Davis was almost crying as he said goodbye, he gave Buck a two shilling piece and hoped he was doing the right thing.

Tom's lorry was smaller and faster than John's but they still travelled along way before he stopped, saying he needed petrol. Pulling into a forecourt, he told George they were on the outskirts of London. He would have to ask a driver in the canteen to give him a lift into the city. Giving Buck a pot of tea and a pie, he sat making out a list of names and places he could choose from with any promise of employment. Buck offered to pay for the pie with the florin John had given him, but was told not to be silly. As Tom left he slipped half crown into Buck's hand.

"I think you are a damned fool" he said "but I wish you the best of luck". Pointing to a chap sitting in the corner, "I have explained your situation, follow him when he leaves". Sitting in the warm canteen, George must have fallen asleep because when he awoke, there were very few people in the cafe and the chap Tom had indicated to him was gone. Picking up his brown paper bag sandwich, he walked outside to see if he could spot him, but there was no one in sight except for a Rolls Royce car with a large parcel strapped to the metal luggage rack, the car was being filled with petrol from the single hand operated pump by the attendant.

The lady passenger opened the window and spoke to the man in a very authoritative voice "put it on his Lordhips account" she commanded. Standing at the rear of the vehicle, Buck thought the driver must be the Lord she was talking about and having an account, they must live nearby, maybe in a village near London, plus they must have money to own a Rolls Royce. When the attendant stopped pumping, the lady rewound her window, the driver started the engine and without thinking for a second he leapt onto the parcel, holding on to the metal luggage rack for dear life.

He had noticed it was eight o'clock when he left the cafe so he must have been travelling for fourteen hours, it was all he could do to hang on when it seemed he could not stand another minute, the road noise changed as the car turned off the highway and onto a gravel drive, then to a stop outside the biggest and the only mansion Buck had ever seen.

An old gentleman in a red waistcoat opened the door for the lady. The driver opened his door to tell the man in the waistcoat to "bring the carpet indoors Thomas".

It was then he was spotted by red waistcoat "I am afraid your Lordship has a stowaway on board sir" he said, holding Bucks arm. His Lordship, in a la di da voice, asked his name and how he came to be there. When Buck had explained his reason for being there the Lord turned to red waistcoat "take him downstairs, Thomas, tell cook to feed him and put him to bed, we will deal with the 'problem' in the morning". Good god Buck thought, in one day he had been promoted from a nothing into a problem.

Downstairs, the hot soup was simply out of this world as was the bread roll and the hot cocoa. The cook showed him into a small room, tucking him up in bed between real clean sheets. He was asleep in ten seconds. Next morning, after an unheard of breakfast of toast and boiled eggs, the red waistcoat arrived to escort him to the Lords study where the 'situation' was to be sorted out.

In one day he had been promoted from a nobody to a problem and now he was a situation, things were sure looking up for George. After being asked a few questions by her Ladyship and Lord Charles, then allowing them to telephone his friend John Davis (who owned the only phone in his home area) for a reference, he was offered yet another promotion of General Factotum to the kitchen.

From a nobody to a General Factotum in one day, whatever next. Buck was really happy and now that he had met Lady Grace and Lord Charles, he felt like that great Wellington boot and the French Neapolitan. One day he declared to himself, 'he' would have a real red waistcoat and buttle her ladyship anytime she needed buttling day or night. From this day forth, this would be his Waterloo. Thank you John Davis.

JIM BURNS AND

J Dyer

I thought once or twice I had spotted the man, although it had been from afar
But now it was real, with that ten gallon hat, he was sitting along in the bar
With slim walking cane and slow dragging walk I watch him crossing the floor
Now I rise to my feet and follow the man not wasting but one second more
Reaching the counter he flips his glass down with a kind of nonchalant air
It travelled so slow as I watched it go, then stop at a maid standing there
"I need a refill" he says to the girl, "And I don't want to pay for the froth
So fill it up slow, keep watch how it flows. Don't stop till it reaches the top"
"Excuse me sir would you allow me" I plead "To pay for your drink as a brother"
"Of course" the man said "And while you are there, give her the price for another"
"I asked for a start could you kindly impart, some great feat not easily found"
"For years my man I have drank at this pub and never once paid for a round"
"Now that is a thing to be proud of" I said "There's a reason you can't tell me why"
"Why not" the man said "I have oodles of friends and idiots like you passing by"
Now I came to the question that many have asked "Excuse me sir, it is that hat"
With a quizzical grin, eyes wandering "Oh I knew it would come round to that"
"It's this saga of Wayne and riding the range, it does make a mans throat so dry"
So I run to the bar and I get a fresh jar, as I reached him, he heaved a long sigh
For hours he filled me with horses and cattle, Mary Rose ships, feats by the score
The famous hat, forget it, was bought from Wayne Thomas, a Welshman next door.

117

GEORGE

J Dyer

Approaching his goal George pauses a while, he stops as he reaches the gate
It's not that he's weary, it's just what he does, it's certain he's not even late
He crosses the car park, a walk through the passage, sidles on up to the bar
To the barmaid he asks for an IPA please, not a glass, but a handle on jar
He's got nothing against the straight glasses, in fact he thinks they are grand
Only he says when they get wet and slippy, they tend to slide out of his hand
If that happened to me says George sadly, watching amber flow cross the floor
Would finish my whole life completely or at best give me heartaches galore
To watch amber liquid flowing from me, see it all disappear down the cracks
I'd have to get treatment for brain drain, or at least give the barmaid the sack
His partner is silent, says nothing at all, with his gaze transfixed straight ahead
"Don't let him kid you" says George with a grin "His eyes swivel round in his head"
"He sits there like a chameleon quite silent, with both his hands gripping that cane
He's a star in his way and might I say has the look of that big bloke John Wayne
You may think he's demised, just follow his eyes, as they wander around to and fro
They can tell him the ones who are friendly and the unfriendly ones have to go.
"He says I am thick as a brick" says George "To say that he should never oughter"
When the reason he gives, I'm sure it's not true, that I had to cross over the water.
Now if I had the brains what he says he has, with the power of speech and the clout
I'd buy a small gun, then have me some fun, by blowing the damn things right out
This mug handle does have its uses that's true, but I tell you there is just one other
If one day I come in, I sit down next to him, he turns and says "Listen hear brother".

SMOKE

Ivy Brown

When Steve and his new girlfriend entered the house they were greeted by his mother, Jane.

"Mum, this is Debbie".

"I've been looking forward to meeting you" said Jane, showing her visitor into the sitting room. Steve stayed in the hallway looking through the post that was on the hallstand.

"I'm popping upstairs for a few minutes" he called, "I need to make a phone call".

"Tell your Grandfather dinner will be in half an hour". Jane turned to her guest "Would you like a sherry"? Debbie accepted, but was amazed when she saw how small the glass was. She would have preferred a drink larger and stronger.

"Is it alright if I smoke"? she asked.

Jane almost dropped the sherry bottle. "It certainly isn't alright. I will not allow anyone to smoke in this house. Can you blame me? It was smoking and drinking that caused my husband's early death. Also, my father has serious breathing problems. Why don't you go out into the garden"?

Debbie agreed. Jane went first into the kitchen to check her cooking and then to the dining room to lay the table. She was soon joined by her son.

"Where's Debbie"? he asked.

"In the garden, smoking" she replied, handing him some cutlery.

"It's a pity you broke up with Lucy. She wasn't very bright, but at least she didn't have any bad habits".

At this point Debbie was making her way back to the sitting room when she overheard the conversation.

"I'm not sure this one's for you" Jane continued. "Apart from smoking I think she's a heavy drinker. I saw the look of disappointment on her face when I handed her a small sherry. But she didn't waste much time gulping it down".

Just then a shuffling noise came from the top of the stairs. Debbie turned to see an elderly man staggering from side to side. She was on her way up to him to ask if he needed help when he lost his balance. She screamed, but managed to grab hold of him.

Jane and Steve heard the scream and came running.

"What's going on?" asked Steve.

"If it hadn't been for the young lady I'd have fallen and broken my neck" said the old man, struggling to get his breath.

They all made their way to the sitting room, Steve attended to his grandfather while Jane checked on Debbie.

"Are you all right"? she asked.

"Yes, just a bit shaky".

"Thank you for saving Dad. I'm sorry I flared up at you. Please forgive me".

"Of course" Debbie laughed "They say there's no smoke without fire".

"Perhaps you should have another cigarette. Steve - get Debbie a glass of Brandy".

"No, thank you" said Debbie. "I don't want either. I've decided to give up my bad habits. I took up smoking and drinking when I started going to the 'Red Lion' with the girls from the office. That's where I met Steve. He was unhappy because he'd just split from his girlfriend. I don't need cigarettes and alcohol now that I've got him". She smiled at him. "She must have been mad to finish with you".

"Thank you" he said, hugging her. "Oh, by the way Mum, one of those letters was from Lucy. She apologised for dumping me and wants us to remain friends".

"You mean she wants you to get back together"? asked Debbie.

"No, she wants us all to go to her wedding, three weeks from this Saturday - make a note of it".

"There's just one thing Debs. You don't need to give up alcohol completely, surely you'll have a glass of champagne to toast the happy couple".

"Oh, I think I can manage that" she laughed "But I promise I won't be getting lit up".

THE HOMECOMING

Maureen O'Sullivan

Family and friends gathered in the large sunlit room. Some waited singly or in small groups on the front drive and others on the patio at the back of the house.

Some were talking in hushed tones. Some sat quietly. One or two paced.

One young girl sat on an old chaise longue under the large front window. Turned sideways, her grey expressionless eyes were glued to the driveway, waiting. Her shoulders were hunched, as if she were cold. Her face was pale as moonlight. Her long thin fingers clutched a gold pen, which she caressed constantly, stroking its well worn surface and passing it from one of her hands to the other, and back again. Her mother crossed to her side and lightly touched her shoulder, smoothing her long brown hair. "He's coming" she whispered.

The girl did not answer, nor move her eyes.

Others stood and began to move outside, as the long black hearse pulled slowly into the driveway, bring him home for one last time.

(1938) JACK ARMSTRONG

J G Dyer

I was seventeen and a miner at the Addison colliery, a small but deep coal mine. Even today, I can sometimes see myself sitting on my haunches at eight o'clock in the morning, my knees entwined with Cappy Dixon's, hunched up, cramped with two others in the bottom deck of a cage at the shaft bottom, waiting to go up.

I was a pony putter which entailed taking empty tubs to the men at the coal face and the full tubs of coal out to the landing or siding. This was gruelling work as the four foot rails were nailed to thin sleepers on uneven ground, with broken props, unsettled roof and not much height or width. From the landing or siding to the shaft bottom, the roadways were widened with twelve foot rails on property sleepers and a walk way, where the tubs arrive in sets of thirty by the haulage system. In turn, where we are working now, would be widened and rails re-laid, this would be the work of Jack Armstrong.

On the day in question, as luck would have it, my last tub of the shift was de-railed badly and as these half ton tubs are not easy to lift back on the rails, I was late getting to the stables. After washing, un-harnessing and bedding the pony, I raced to the bottom gate of the cage and called out for him to wait "You're lucky, there is room for one more" he said. Head lowered, my knees entwining with Cappies, I bent double to get in.

The on-setter, Bobby Humble was pressing the steel barred gate against me, closing it as I squeezed in. I saw him pushing the bolt in, but before he could engage the locking pin, the cage left with a huge jerk, unlike the ordinary lift we were used to.

I suppose we had passed the half way mark when there were screeching and grinding noises at the side of the cage, sparks were flying in front of Cappy and myself, then the cage shuddered to a sudden stop. Beside us four, there were six men in the top deck, four standing, with two kneeling between their legs, one of them asked if we could see anything, but like the others, we had emptied our carbide lamps down below, we were all in the dark. I put my hand out to try and feel something, but there was nothing to feel. I called up to them that the gate was gone. The top deck was full of old timers which I suppose made us feel a bit safer.

"Run your hand around outside and see what you can feel, but not too far" said a voice from above, this I did very slowly. I found the gate at my side was all tangled up like a ball between the cage and somewhere else, it must have sprung open. I reported this to the old men above. "Keep still" the voice said "They will know something is wrong, just stay quiet" I cannot recall the names of the other two lads who were there, but I can recall Cappy, he was the one who talked a lot, but now he was the only one crying and moaning, but like the others I was scared stiff.

We did not know how long we had sat, when suddenly we heard the chains and the butterfly rattle down on to the top of the cage and then a slithering sound. A voice from the top deck yelled out "The stupid bastards are lowering the rope hoping the cage will break free, all together now, yell for them to stop". We began yelling and screaming for them above to STOP. "Is it still moving" the voice asked, I put my hand out very slowly, the greasy rope was still moving, I was about to report it when the voice above said "Don't worry son, I can feel it now and its going up thank heaven".

We heard the chains rattle on top of the cage again and then a slight jerk as the rope tightened on the butterfly. We heard them talking above, stating that even if the cage had freed itself, it would have certainly snapped the rope and gone to the bottom. Again they warned us to sit still. No-one had a watch, so we had no idea how long we had been there and if we did, no-one had a light to see it with. Someone asked if we should shout, but the old hands above told us that 'they', whoever 'they' were, knew we were here and would think of some way to get us up. Our legs were aching in that cramped place and once I scared myself to death because at one point, I was certain I had fallen asleep. As the shaft also acted as an airway to the workings down below, it was very cold and had this happened in the winter time, no-one could have helped us, because in the winter a brazier of coke was burnt day and night to stop the shaft from freezing up.

The old man in the upper deck again asked us to keep quiet, he thought he had heard something, I myself thought I had heard a scraping sound and prayed that the rope was not being lowered again. The same voice spoke "We can see a light coming".

It seemed ages before we also saw the flash, then someone was talking to the top deck men. They were telling him what we had said about the gate being jammed. Then the man was in front of Cappy and me "Won't be long now lads" it was Jack Armstrong. He wore a harness and safety rope, the man had climbed down the shaft between timber baulks and guide rails with tools tied to his waist, his lamp clearly showed the steel barred gate wrapped like a football between the corner of the cage and the side of the shaft. Jack took a hack saw from the bag and began to cut at the metal. It seemed years before we heard pieces pinging as they fell, striking the sides of the shaft. We watched him as he knelt on the shaft timbers, working hard with that hacksaw, then my heart almost stopped. The cage gave a groan and shook as it broke free from the tangled gate, we heard the metal bouncing off the sides as it fell to the shaft bottom. Jack told us all to sit tight, he was going to take his harness off and ride up on top of the cage. He called out for a lift and then we were moving. The cage stopped at ground level, this was used for slinging ponies, or large objects, where Jack had been lowered from and where he was to leap off. We could hear the voices of the local people who had gathered at the pit head cheering as the cage was raised to exit the six men above us, this seemed to take for ever, we were yelling for them to hurry, but at last it was our turn. We found the reason why it had taken so long to get out, we could not move our legs, it was so painful, the men and women had to drag us out one by one and sit us on chairs. We were bent rigid, even the ones who had been standing in the cage had collapsed in a heap. The women had made tea, which was much appreciated. The manager told us that the time was now two fifteen, we had been hanging in the shaft for more than six hours. With lots of massage and a couple of aspirin tablets, we were painfully able to rise and move around, all we wanted to do now was to go home. Old Jack Armstrong was standing by himself at the rear as we left.

Each of us went across in turn and hugged old Jack. Without speaking a word, he knew how thankful we all were and if he ever needed us we would be there for him.

Jack Armstrong, he was fifty four years of age, what a man.

PS. Jack was the rope splicer, track layer, engineer and anything else. I am unaware that he got any recognition for his action, but we all got the next night off (unpaid) to recuperate. When eventually I arrived home (I was not married at the time) they had not even heard about the mishap, no-one asked why I had turned up at half past three in the afternoon, instead of eight thirty in the morning. Maybe they thought I had worked a double shift. How I wished I had eaten that food.

There was a court hearing, at which the management wanted to blame the on-setter with negligence, but Cappy and I swore in court that he was nowhere near the bell when the cage left and he was cleared. The rope winding drum or the engineer was to blame.

PPS. The 'butterfly' is a safety device which, should anything happen to the winding gear, to prevent the cage being drawn over the big wheels on the pit head.

Below the wheels of the pit head and above the butterfly on the rope, a safety ring of metal is firmly set, should the winder over reach, the rope shackle enters the ring which in turn closes the butterfly and releases the said shackle and rope. The freed cage then falls back 'hopefully' onto four keeps, which is supposed to stop it from plunging to the bottom of the said shaft. This, to my knowledge has never happened and I pray it never does.

BLACK & WHITE

Beryl Risbridger

"You really make me sick. I've never come across anyone more judgemental than you" Bob said with almost clenched teeth. "You are never willing to listen to anyone else's point of view. With you, everything is either black or white, but even then that depends on your own point of view".

"That's because I'm always right" replied Jack, somewhat tongue in cheek.

"Are you really so thick skinned that you don't know what people say about you behind your back"?

As usual, Jack came back with one of his facetious remarks, he was always very quick witted and despite himself, Bob had to give a grin, he couldn't help liking his friend.

"See you later at the pub, Jack"?

"Ok mate" and he walked away.

Later on, shaving himself, Jack looked at his reflection in the mirror and said to himself "how wrong you are Bob, if only you knew what a fraud I am. You think I am so sure of myself and I do have to admit I do put on a good performance in public, but I really have no confidence in myself".

Over the years he had built an invisible wall around himself, protecting himself from the past before he ended up here.

From the age of five he had been in a Children's Home, his parents having been killed in a car crash - at least that was what he had been told. He hadn't been unhappy in the Home, nor had he been happy. He always felt that Mr &Mrs Duncan, who ran the Home, seemed to be watching him more than the other children in their care. If he did anything wrong, even if it wasn't his fault, he always seemed to get the blame.

So far as he knew, he had no living relatives, but one day a woman arrived asking to see him. She spent a long time with Mr & Mrs Duncan in their office, while he waited outside. Eventually he was called in and told that this lady was his Father's half sister who was over from Australia on a holiday.

She had always known that she had a Nephew somewhere in England, but had never been in a position before to trace him. Having different surnames had made it even more difficult. She asked the Duncans if she could take him to the Village for tea, giving them time to talk and perhaps get to know each other a little. Jack instantly liked her and knowing he had at least one relative made him feel different.

Sadly, Auntie Sue, as she told him to call her, was at the end of her trip and was returning home, but she told Jack that they must stay in touch..

For a few years they wrote once a month, but when Jack reached 14 she contacted the Authorities for permission to let him come and live with her in Australia, which was granted. She sent him the fare and he arrived in Perth, where he settled happily.

One day he overheard Auntie Sue talking to her friend on the phone and something was mentioned about the Parents. Jack asked his Aunt repeatedly what it was, but all she would say that it was a long time ago and best left alone, which made him more and more curious.

One day he and Auntie Sue's son got into an argument and his Cousin said something in anger that Jack wished he'd never found out.

It seemed that his Parents hadn't died in a car crash, but that his Father, who apparently had a violent temper, had become angry with his Mother and had accidentally killed her, for which he was sent to Prison and eventually, unable to live with his guilt, had killed himself.

Jack was, of course, devastated and this was the beginning of him building his invisible wall. When he arrived back in England, everyone accepted that he had been orphaned because of a car crash.

He had often been tempted to tell Bob, who was his best friend, the real reason why he had got his reputation, but decided it was easier to be known as the pig headed bloke who could only see things as black or white, never grey, but perhaps he would, one day feel he didn't have to hide behind his reputation any longer.

RING A ROSES

John Rogers

At the end of the Second World War money was very tight. Service men being demobilised from the Services were given the bare necessities to tide them over till they found work in Civvy Street. Some thousands of them opted to marry the sweethearts that had waited for them. In those days there was only one barely

affordable wedding ring, nine carat gold, the rest brass. That invariably lasted right up to one of the important anniversaries when the male invariably received a more elaborate ring from his spouse.

Charlie was one of those, he got his flash very chunky one of twenty two carat on his twenty fifth anniversary and right proud he was of it too. After a visit one year to the Chelsea Flower

Show, he fell in love with roses. Most of his time was spent pruning, deadheading, spraying, his latest craze, by his twenty sixth, the ring had gone.

His wife was annoyed and suspicious for old Charlie liked a smoke and a drink and bearing in mind the amount of money he was spending on roses and in the pub, she had her doubts.
"You haven't got the best one of them all" he shouted, Ena Harnes.

"S, up by the water barrel she is"
Impatiently Minnie bustled back up the garden. As she cut a couple of those beautiful full red roses, a glint from one of the old spurs caught her eye. Sure enough it was the ring. She never said a word.
On the big day Charlie got a present from Minnie. When he opened it here was the ring, brand spanking new.
"My God girl, you've bought another".
To which his son replied "you silly old bugger, it is the same one.
We had it polished, now perhaps you will take proper care of it".
Charlie gave up smoking, but not drinking.

SNOW FLAKES

Lewis Button

As he switched on his headlights he saw the first few snow flakes fall. He thought how pretty they looked, like delicate pieces of some fabric designed by the Gods. He was driving along the M62 from Manchester towards Leeds. He had heard the heavy snow warnings, but he had to go and it did not look as though it was going to settle. Tom's mother had had a seizure and had to be admitted to St Jimmies, as it was known colloquially, he knew of course she would receive the best attention in this world wide famous hospital.

After driving a few miles, the once pretty flakes were coming down at an alarming rate and it began to look as though the weather forecast was accurate. The wind was now gusting and the snow fall became heavier, in fact the windscreen wipers had to work overtime to clear the screen when he saw ahead a flashing light and was pulled over. The motorway is closed ahead he was informed, take the next exit and follow the detour signs for the next few miles then you will be able to return to the main road system. Tom saw the sign, albeit a little late and went into a semi skid, managed to right the car and went into the town of Rottenstall. Now who would name a town thus he thought, some Lancastrian with a perverted sense of humour.

His mobile started to ring, it was the hospital, his mother had taken a turn for the worse and it was imperative that he came as quickly as possible in order to see her. Tom gritted his teeth, he was going along at about 15mph and when he did try to accelerate the car did not hold the road very well, so he would do the best he could. Rottenstall lived up to it's name as he drove through he thought, even under a layer of snow it still looked dirty and unkempt. He saw a sign ahead, 24 hour Esso Petrol, looked at his dashboard and realised that although under normal conditions he had enough petrol, in these circumstances he had better fill up and as he skidded to a halt, he saw the office was empty and the station was unattended. He looked at the pumps and saw there was a self serve facility on the pumps, he inserted the card, but it was rejected. Suddenly out of the snowy night a hooded young man appeared politely asked if he could help, took his card, snatched his phone, kicked him in the groin and disappeared into the night.

This journey was turning into his worst nightmare, but there was yet more to come. Shaken, he followed the detour signs and was soon back on the motorway which had now been cleared by the snowploughs. There was now blizzard conditions to contend with. He was now doing about 30 mph when he thought he could see the shadow of a lorry or something ahead with flashing lights. Too late he realised that there was a hold up ahead, he went into a skid, hit the nearside of the lorry, went off the road into a field after being hit by the car behind. The airbag exploded into life crushing his ribs and he passed out. After what seemed an eternity he saw a torch light shining into his car, a policeman grunted something about don't bother with this one, he's probably dead. I'm not, I'm not, I tried to say, but nothing came out. My ribs felt crushed and my eyes would not open, how could I let them know, I passed out again.

Jack Daniels, or whisky as his friends knew him, had just come on duty when the alarm call had come in to Blue Watch, Leeds Central Fire Station. He bent over the car to release the supposed corpse. Hey, he called, this guy's alive you know. He's got a faint pulse, only about 35 so he is just about hanging on. The paramedics rushed over and started work on Tom. What's his name he asked the fireman? I think it might be Tom, that's the name on his car keys. Wake up Tom, said the nurse! Tom was aware what was going on in his semi comatose state. He could see the snow flakes gently floating around and settling on the man's face. It looked slightly comic and he would have smiled if he were able. Tom found out he could talk, St James he said, what did he say? Said the fireman. It sounded like St James to me said the paramedic. Tom tried again, St Jimmies, a little louder. Bugger me, he's coming through it, I thought he was a goner, he is some lucky sod that you saw he was alive. Yes mate, that's where we are taking you. Tom tried to smile, not too successfully.

At St James Hospital, Tom's sister Vera and his ex wife were visiting his mother and really waiting for the end. They had been sent for and told to fear the worst, when a nurse came in and told them of Tom's accident and how bad he was. They were whispering at the bedside not realising that mother could hear every word. What's wrong, what's the matter with my Tom. The girls replied he's ok, he had a slight accident, but he is alright. Don't lie to me said the old lady and she started to panic. Mum, he is alright, he's coming to see you here. This seemed to placate the old lady. She started to make an unexpected recovery. The nurse came into the side ward and could not believe her eyes to see the old girl sitting up in bed as large as life. Where's my boy, she barked at the nurse, the girl just smiled in disbelief. We are just doing some tests and then he will be admitted to a ward. I

want to see him, she snapped again. As soon as he's admitted you shall, answered the nurse. The two sisters in law just grimaced to the nurse who shrugged her shoulders and smiled. An hour went by, which seemed like an eternity and the nurse came back. We'll take you to see him if you think you're up to it. Before you could say Jack Robinson, she was out of the bed and into a wheelchair, being pushed through the busy corridors. She looked at her son lying there in a dazed state and shouted at him, whatever possessed you to go out in that blooming snow, you must be touched or something. I've always hated snow she snapped.

Oh Mum, thought Tom, you are a bloody miracle. I was coming to see you and in the end you came to see me.

THE NEW ARRIVAL

Jim Burns

The Diaspora from London started after the 1939-45 war. London County Council built satellite towns around London, Stevenage, Harlow, Debden, Hainault. The breakup of communities are still felt today.

Then it was my turn, a letter from the Tower Hamlets Council offered me an exchange to Hainault. The excitement was overwhelming, no more bugs, no more stink from the gas works and blocked up dust sheets. The problem was, where was Hainault. I knew it was at the end of the line according to the underground map.

We, my wife and four kids, arrived on a bright sunny day to view the house. I told the kids to play on the large green while we looked over the house. Then a loud voice from the house opposite "You are not parking your car there, I've been parking there for ten years", "sorry" I replied. Then another voice further down, "No ball games on the grass, its on the notice board". Come on kids, "welcome to semi detached suburbia" I said to my wife.

Roaming through the rooms, I was apprehensive, the Council decorators had not finished, every room a mess, the garden a jungle, rusty bikes, car parts strewn around. The voices of our potential new neighbours in my head "No, I don't like it" I said to my wife "I don't feel comfortable".

We handed the keys back to the Council Office. It was 4 o'clock. We went to visit my brother who lived at the other end of the estate. After talking, he convinced me to take the offer up. It was 5 o'clock when we arrived at the Council Office. They were closing for the weekend, we got the keys back and waited for a letter to tell us to move.

LONELINESS IS THE BEDMATE OF THE GRAVE

Wandering the desert of Hainault, like a migrant in a new country, pub after pub looking for like minded people. Then drinking in the Alfreds Head, I saw an old workmate. My face lit up "Hello Fred, I didn't know you lived in Hainault". Putting my beer on his table and pulling a chair up "Yeah, I moved about five years ago, started my own bagging business up" Fred said. "That's great, do you come here often" I asked. "No, not often, there is a saying in Hainault, friendly, but not too friendly". "Thanks for the advice Fred" picking my beer up and moved to the other bar.

Then there was a light at the end of the tunnel, I joined the Hainault Working Mans Club, made a friend of the Secretary.

We went to Redbridge evening classes 'Creative Writers', formed a writers group at the Club, printed and published our first book called 'Hainault The End of the Line'.

Now after twenty years and six books printed and published and still going strong.

I now realize that Hainault was not the end of the line, but a new beginning.

BIRD WATCH
A.S.A.

A gentle Dove, immaculately dressed.
Flies in to feed as though its been possessed,
Loud rustling wings and raucous cry,
With an unearthly scream it drops out from the sky.
Scattering Sparrows on the ground
Then feeding, it makes not another sound.

A Blue Tit flits from nuts to fat
We sit, watching this natural acrobat.
He lands right way up, upside down
Any which way will do.
A lively bundle of coloured feathers
An entertainer too?

A Robin sings, into the sun lit sky,
Its' scarlet breast catches on the eye
He moves around so quickly
Much faster than you think.
One second he's there before you
Then disappears
Much quicker than you can wink.

IT WASN'T FUNNY AT THE TIME..........

Maureen O'Sullivan

Matthew can't survive without his mobile telephone. He uses it for business mainly so it is always important that calls are answered promptly! It is a state-of-the-art design, with all sorts of special functions, including a 'hands free' which means that you can have a conversation without actually placing the telephone to your ear. It also means that voices come over loud and clear, even at a distance. So it is even more vital to ensure that the telephone is switched off when you don't want to be disturbed.

Like on the day of Matthew's grandfather's funeral!

Matthew, being the eldest grandson, was in the forefront carrying his grandfather's coffin. He, on the right hand side and his first cousin, Simon, on the left hand side were the 'pacemakers' for the ones to follow. "Their grandfather would be so proud" was whispered more than once by loving mothers, wiping away tears, as the six handsome young men in their dark suits, white shirts and black ties, walked with dignity into the church and proceeded along the very long aisle. The organ played sombre music in the background.

Out of the blue, the solemnity was broken by a voice which echoed loudly around the lofty walls. People looked around and at each other questioningly. The voice appeared to have come from inside the coffin!

"How much longer are you likely to be? I'm bloody uncomfortable waiting here for you".

"Shhhhh" came from someone close by.

"Never mind Shhhhh" the loud voice continued, "you said you'd pick me up for the funeral, so where are you"?

A mutter came from somewhere.

"What's that you said"? the voice asked. "Speak up man, I can't hear you".

"I'm carrying the coffin", growled Matthew from between his teeth, completely unable to take either hand away from the coffin or from his cousin's shoulder to switch off his mobile phone. "So for God's sake shut up".

It wasn't funny at the time.........but we did laugh afterwards! And Matthew's grandfather would also have laughed.

A MUSEUM PIECE

Marion Osborn

The oldest thing that I own is myself and that is what I am bringing to you today. The proof of my antiquity is my birth certificate; my bus pass verifies its authenticity. I well remember showing it to a bus driver once and his comment "Put it away, it's the worst one I've seen"! to the merriment of my fellow passengers.

But I digress, my 'provenance', in antique professional jargon, is probably worth more than my intrinsic value, for I have lived many lives. I was born on exactly the same date as the Queen. There the similarity ends, unfortunately. Well, for starters I have had more husbands than she's had children. Namely five, yes I did say five and have outlived all of them except for my current toy boy Jason. My body's a bit of a marriage as well. I've had four face-lifts, as well as a liver transplant, after which I had to knock the drinking on the head. Ruined my social life that did, well Vichy water is so dull!

In my younger days I was a bit of a girl and did the rounds of the music halls singing and dancing. Made a fair living, but it did my knees in and had to have them replaced. Anyone who says anything different is a liar, for I was never in Northern Ireland, well only once when visiting my Auntie Bridget during the troubles. When we fled, I mean came back to England, I had my hips done on the NHS. Hardly any of me is original when I come to think of it, but what there is choice! I am afraid that I have no hallmarks and my patina fades to a sickly paleness in winter. Nonetheless I am a genuine antique, for with the shipment of antiques abroad and the resultant scarcity, eighty is today's one hundred.

If I was put up for auction and didn't reach my reserve price and remained unsold, the humiliation would be hard to bear. No, I

135

would much rather my descendants donated me to a museum. But if on the other hand, I reached an unprecedented amount, with discerning buyers vying each other for the privilege of owning me - ah that would be rapture indeed! The joy of all eyes on yours truly - first one bid then another. Mounting higher and higher. The rivalry, the passion, the desire. Such feelings unleashed in a simple Auction Room by little old me! Down to the final two, then one shakes his head, unable to go on and then the gavel goes down. Sold! The chagrin and disappointment of the loser and the triumph of the winner. And I go to the worthy victor. Power and money combined. Powerful aphrodisiacs indeed.

And my future? Well who knows, in the fullness of time and after a little more restoration, I might even get to meet my maker!

PRACTICE TO DECEIVE
John Rogers

My heart bleeds for the Banksters'
In all their misery,
Having to apologise to everyone
On prime time TV
They no doubt negotiated their bonuses
Before the show began
To give the false idea that each is an honest man.
Unfortunately their predatory methods
Leave a lot to be desired
The callous way they fleece their prey
Is but greed inspired
There is no cure! I am afraid the only one we've got
All errant bankers should be taken out and shot.

AYE AYE MAN
(As eye)

J G Dyer

This is and always has been the greeting of northern miners on the meeting of each other aye-aye which means 'how are you' and is answered by a long drawn out single ayee in recognition, except on this particular morning it seemed different to Tom. He was going out-bye (towards the shaft and home) at the end of his shift, meeting his 'Marra' (Partner) Jack half way as they always did, to exchange views as to the condition of the coal face and of safety. "Aye-aye Tom" said Jack. "Ayee" replied Tom. "Anything the matter Jack" with a look of askance on his face.

"Why no" was the answer "should there be?".Tom looked at his mate's face in the light of his lamp. "It's just the way you said aye-aye, as if you were short of breath". Jack tapped his steel capped pit boots with his pick blade "You mean as if it had a hyphen in it".

There was a worried look on Tom's face "What is a hyphen Jack, you're not sick are you?". Jack smiled in the gloom of the gallery "I'm ok Tom, a hyphen just joins words together, something like a split infinitive, don't worry about it". They exchanged their views about the condition at the coal face etc then parted. "Take care Tom" said Jack "Ayee and you take care" answered Tom,

still with that worried look on his face. Jack went in to work, Tom left for home, fretting about his friend.

On reaching the shaft bottom and waiting for the cage to go up to the surface, he caught hold of the cage man. "Did my mate Jack speak to you when he came down, was he alright". The man answered "Yes, he said aye-aye, he seemed ok". He opened the cage door. Still worried, Tom went on. "Did he say aye-aye with a hyphen do you think?" Holding the gate, he stared at Tom. "How the hell do I know if he had a hyphen, get in the cage".

Tom got in, the bell rang and he was jerked upwards. Still not happy, Tom arrived at the lamp cabin, he unbuckled the battery from his belt and held it up to the lamp man, who looked quizzically at Tom. "What's up man, you look worried". Tom gave a puzzled smile "Did you speak to my mate Jack?" As he took Tom's lamp, he replied "Yes, he said aye-aye as I gave him his lamp and token". Tom reached in and grabbed his arm. "Do you think he had a hyphen when he said aye-aye?". The lamp man pulled his arm away "Go home Tom, go to bed, you must be tired".

Tom was still fretting about his partner as he walked home. I know he thought, his wife will know how he is, she only lives a few doors away, I'll call on my way home and ask her. This was long before pit baths were installed and Tom was black with coal dust, but although it was still dark, Sally, Jack's wife, would not mind him calling. He climbed the three steps of number nine and proceeded to rattle the handle of the stout door. Jack's wife, who was busy cleaning the oven and fender rose from the floor,

proceeded to the door and opened it. She let out an ear piercing scream as she was confronted by the black faced Tom standing there. She slumped to the floor blubbering and shaking like a leaf.

Tom helped her to her feet, she clung to him "Oh God, please Tom tell me he's not dead" she sobbed "Tell me he's alright Tom, where is he Tom".

She was sobbing, gripping his lapels. Tom held her against the wooden screen. "Jack's alright Sally, don't cry, Jack's in the pit, he's ok, only you see I am a bit worried about him". Sally stared into Tom's eyes.

"Why are you worried, what do you mean, tell me". Tom looked at her "When Jack said aye-aye as he left this morning, do you think he had a hyphen in the way he said it".

Sally stood there glaring at him. "You damned idiot" she yelled, "You numbskull, you hammer on my bloody door, you scare me half out of my wits with your black face, thinking my Jack is lying buried down there, then you have the stupid gall to ask me if my Jack has a hyphen. If I knew what a bloody hyphen was, I would brain you with it, if you ever had any brains". She slammed the door shut which made Tom fall down the three steps.

When he arrived home, Tom had a wash in the tin bath, then after explaining to his wife why he was late and why he was worried, he asked her if she ever had a hyphen when she breathed. His wife smiled as she slowly explained to her husband what a hyphen was, plus the split infinitive. Tom was so relieved when he went to bed, he slept like a log. That night he got ready for work and went whistling down to the mine. He met his friend at the usual place and as they met, he called out to his partner

"Aye-aye Jack" then proceeded to give him a full blooded punch to the stomach, a long winded Ayeea came from Jack "Tom, what the bloody hell was that for" he gasped. "Well" said Tom most nonchalantly as he sat down. "That is what you might like to tell your Sally is an eye for an eye without a hyphen, or even a split infinitive ok"

IN A WORD Metaphor

J G Dyer

I took home a word that was told me and it really did cause quite a stir
My young sister said that she had the CD recorded by Sonny and Cher
My brother says that's utter nonsense, in the navy, he's quite Jack the lad
That's how ships talk to each other he said, by waving two bright coloured flags
Quite surprised when Aunt Ada injected, she just visits for one day or two
It's that thing what the doctor is using she said, when people can't go to the loo
We all have a laugh at poor Ada so much so, she gives out a wild shriek
Don't laugh she screamed cause I've had it, I couldn't sit down for a week
Grandad, he just sits there grinning, my god, he says, you are such fools
Of course it's a doctor's thingy alright, for stiffening old pensioner's tools
Tommy next door, now he's entered and he'd listened to all of us shout
The're nothing he said, when you've METAPHOR, the're nothing to write home about
We went down to the pub, we met Charlie, much travelled, both near and far
METAPHOR he says, a city in India, I've been there, near old Zanzibar
The barmaid was puzzled, "Who Meta-for-what? To me it is all double Dutch
Let the barn-cake who told you say what it is, seeing as he knows so much".

139

POETS CORNER

Beryl Risbridger

With a great deal of trepidation, Margot tentatively pushed open the door of the pub.

"How could I have let myself be talked into doing this" she thought to herself, I've never been into a pub on my own!"

As she entered she felt every eye had turned to look at her, although she knew this was completely stupid because it was so noisy with the groups chattering away, that no one even knew she was there. Every instinct told her to turn round and go out again, but she faintly heard her name being called and glancing back she saw an outstretched arm waving her to the far end of the bar.

"That's torn it" she thought "I can't escape now".

Fixing a nervous smile on her face, she edged her way over to the group where her friend Janet was. Janet introduced her, but to Margot they were just a sea of faces. Everyone seemed very pleasant and friendly, but Margot was so nervous she just smiled, but was unable to join in the conversation.

Standing on a seat and clapping loudly a man was, somehow, able to bring the whole bar to silence and Margot was amazed how he had managed it.

"It's now 8 o'clock and I imagine that everyone who is coming is now here, so I think we should start. Have all the groups got the list of the order of readings? Good. So I suggest that No.1 who are the Representatives from the Local Authority Group start us off".

There were polite claps as the Group made their way to the microphone. One by one they read their poems, some rhyming and some in blank verse.

Margot found herself relaxing and began to enjoy the very varied selection that every group had produced. Some were extremely good, some amusing and others almost incomprehensible!!

Then it was her groups turn. Apart from Janet, whose Writing Group it was, she knew no one else, but Janet had been trying for ages to persuade her to come to one of their meetings as she felt Margot had real talent, but was too shy to show her work to anyone else.

"I'll stay here and listen to you all" said Margot, but Janet was not having any of this, it had taken her so long to have got to this stage and she wasn't going to let Margot slip away yet again.

Without realising how it had happened, Margot found herself up with the rest of the group and one by one they performed, but what they said Margot couldn't say, she was too petrified to even hear.

The MC announced that they had a new, very nervous writer in their midst and would we give her a big welcome. Somehow Margot was at the mike, looking at a sea of faces. She focused on a girl at the front with a kind, smiling face, doing her best to encourage Margot. Very quietly and hesitantly, Margot began. The smiling face nodded encouragingly and suddenly Margot found her voice, which was a very pleasant one, lost her nervousness and performed as though she was alone and no one else could hear.

When she had finished, there was a burst of genuine clapping in appreciation. Janet gave her a big hug and Margot came down to Earth. For a short time she had no longer been her normal shy, retiring self.

All Janet's group were so complimentary and Margot felt she was accepted and wanted. She joined the group and looked forward to their meetings and especially to the various Poets Corners they were invited to and from that time in her life, she felt she belonged. It was a great feeling.

ONE HAS TO START SOMEWHERE

John Rogers

Many sighs have passed under the bridge since I was born. This momentous event took place some eighty five years ago.

The small herring fishing town on the south east coast of Ireland was ill prepared for this momentous event.

There were two much divided factions in the town, from Oliver Cromwell in bygone days, the Iron Rings of stabled horses in the Roman Catholic Churches are a very poignant reminder.

Those two schools of thought still remain the Anglophiles and the Patriots.

Into this maelstrom of controversy I arrived very much unwanted.

My Mother's family depended on English money; my Father was a patriot (never the twain should have met). They did and I was the unfortunate result.

She was barely fifteen, he was twenty. A bit of a gadabout, actor, singer and very brave Irishman? With not one iota of what Fatherhood meant.

I was told that on one of his rare appearances after I was born, he heard me mewling in the corner. He questioned "What is that bloody noise?" On being told "That is your son!", he replied callously "Throw a bloody sack over it".

For all his dislike of the English, he was very proud of the exploits of his own Father, a sailor in the British Navy who died on HMS Indefatiguable in 1916 at Jutland. His name was Bartholomew and that was the only gift bestowed upon me by my errant parent. He died when I was six. I never really bonded with my Mother, because of her husband's roving eye and desertion, she was obliged to farm me out to the cheapest foster person she could find during those first six years.

He died in the house where I was born. I was there downstairs listening to him calling my Mother Betty in a mournful voice. (I realize in writing this, I never actually saw my Father alive and that was the only time I ever heard him) he passed away within the hour.

I remember I got nine pennies from the people there. On leaving, my Mother said she would look after them for me. That was the last I saw of them. That night was to be a turning point in my life. As we both left the house of death it was very late, a terrific howling and screaming could be heard in the velvet blackness. Mother said it was the Banshees, as you can imagine I was terrified.

We ended up outside a tiny terraced house in a long street at about midnight. She knocked on the door and a big fat man with a grey moustache let us in.

It was her Father, known as Captain John Doyle of the Irish Lights. He and his two sons had spent their lives on lighthouses and light ships. He became my family. He fostered me for some five years and I grew to love and respect him to such a degree that it nearly broke my heart, when one night he sat me on his knee and holding a clock in his hand he said "Now son, look at them hands. When they go round to here you will be with your Mother in England". I believe I cried all night.

That wonderful man had been diagnosed with cancer and knew he was dying. He passed away within three months, I still miss, love and respect him in every sorrowful memory. He gave me an understanding of values that only a good and capable counsellor could. In fact people used to come into his sitting room for just that purpose. He had been retired for many years. On the landing of his two up, two down was a wooden chest holding all his gold braided uniforms. I used to plead with him to put them on and I was so proud when he did with all the gold braid and shiny buttons. I do believe that my admiration embarrassed him.

That house is still there in a place called The Faythe, Co Wexford. It is such a tiny place, the parlour was his place for consultation, a tiny room on the right down the passage. When I first lived there, we had a dry toilet in the yard.

Granda had a flush toilet built under the stairs just past the parlour in the passage. I can visage him sitting there, his trousers round his ankles, the only privacy being the acrid smoke from his pipe of strong smelling tobacco.

When he went to his Harriers Club some evenings, I used to let my playmates in to pull the chain on the payment of one sweet per pull; I guess we must have nearly emptied the local reservoir. His youngest son John lived just across the road from us. Granda never spoke to him, for John had married a divorcee with two young daughters from her previous marriage.

I had a high regard for John, he fascinated me.

When the old man was at the Club, John with my help used to raid his vegetable garden. I think Granda knew.

I was told when I was taken from Ireland, I would be eaten alive by the English. Obviously I did not taste good and after seventy five years I must have deteriorated even more, so I feel pretty safe now.

It took me thirty five years, a wife and two sons to get back to Ireland. England by the grace has been good to me.

So as it was in the beginning, so it shall be WORD without end.

Ahem! I am a man of all people now.

SAD HUMOUR
A.S.A.

Yer know we can't be happy all the time, we all feel sad on occasions, but I ave me own recipe to get over it. I goes darn ter the church weather permitting of course, sit on a bench and look at the gargles, you know, those little faces carved all over, they had a sense of yomour those old Masons when they carved em. They were representations of people who lived in ter Villige and blow me if they still don't, even though they were carved a cuppla undred years ago. That ones loike the Landlord of the Duck and Fox and going round I can pick out the faces of most of em in the Village, but the one oi loike is that old Devils face that gives me a right old laugh, it's just loike my missis, oh I do laugh.

A FISHY STORY

Maureen O'Sullivan

Dear Sir,

I gotta complaint about your fish.

I bought some cod in your store on Friday. Right expensive it were too. That night I got it ready, dipped it in egg and breadcrumbs like what I normally do and stuck it in the pan. As it started to cook, I noticed one or two what looked like bones sticking out. I hadn't noticed them before. I went to pull them out and to my horror they moved and squiggled out of my hand. They were worms! Long, white worms! Well, I nearly threw up there and then. I screamed me head off and me husband came running into the kitchen. He were none too pleased as he was watching the horse racing.

"Oh my Lord" says he, "whatever have you done?"

"I ain't done nothing" I said, "but look at the fish".

"What's wrong with it?" he said

"What's wrong with it?" I says, "can't you see the worms?"

"Worms, worms, have you gone off your head woman?" he said

"See for yourself" I said, poking at them with a fork. By then they were starting to cook so weren't so lively.

Anyways, I put the fish, worms and all in a plastic box and took them back to your shop. I saw the fishmonger and what you think he said?

"It's quite normal" says he, "lots of cod have worms and some other fish too. If you buy them frozen, the worms would be dead and you'd be none the wiser".

"None the wiser!" I said. I never heard the like. Not even an apology, just "it's quite normal".

Well, I want some compensation. There's the cost of the fish, the ruination of our evening - we had to have beans on toast for dinner. My husband won't ever eat fish again, so where does that leave me on Fridays? - trying to think of something else to dish up.

No-one I've spoken to ever heard of fish with worms. Cats and dogs with worms, yes, but fish! My neighbour Fred's a fisherman and he said he uses worms for bait and maybe the fish swallowed the worms, but his worms are little, like maggots, so I don't think that's the case.

I rang the Town Hall and they put me through to some 12 year old in Training Standards or somethink, who didn't know what I was talking about, so I got no joy there. So it's up to you!

I've been coming to your shop for over 30 years, but won't come no more unless you do something about this. It's right upset my husband. He has an ulcer and it's flared right up with the stress of it. He's going to see the doctor. I can't sleep at night. I keep seeing those horrible white worms. We might have to see a solicitor.

Fred said I ought to ring the Ilford Recorder. I'll wait to hear what you have to say first.

Yours disgustingly of Hainault.

THE REUNION

Marion Osborn

Quo vadis. 'Whither goest thou' I asked myself as I hurtled down the motorway towards Lester's Leisure Centre for the Reunion. Driving me there was an old classmate who for the life of me I couldn't remember. And to make matters worse, when I'd got into her car she'd asked.

"Now be honest, do you remember me?"

"Er, oh dear" I'd stammered, not wanting to offend her, but honesty prevailing, I went on "I feel awful, er, actually no".

But she'd only laughed, disregarding my embarrassment, saying "Don't worry about it".

But me being me, I did. Why oh why had I agreed to go! It had all started about two years prior when I'd been chatting to Pauline in my Art Group and had discovered that she had attended the same school as me, but not at the same time, as she was much younger. She then brought in a magazine that the school published each year and lo and behold my name was in it. "Could Maria Ramos contact us". I couldn't believe it. So I made contact and was told there was a reunion being organized and did I want to come.

And so here I was. But as it had got nearer to the date, I'd almost chickened out by saying I wouldn't be able to get to the rendezvous, as I couldn't drive. Well, it was near Brighton! But my excuse had been pulled out from beneath me. Jodie Brown and I couldn't recall anyone of that name in my class, who lived in Barking, a stones throw away, could take me.

A fortnight before the due date, she had kindly taken me out for a coffee so we could meet, as she'd realized it could be very daunting for me. I hadn't seen any of my old school mates for fifty two years, when I was a very tiny sixteen year old, white ankle socked and gym slipped girl. Probably looking like a very immature eleven year old of today. She'd brought one of the other girls with her, Susan Makepeace, who I at least remembered and vaguely recognized. I thought I'd carried off the meeting quite well and that Jodie hadn't fallen into the fact that I hadn't known her from Adam, but obviously not. Halfway there we pulled in at a pub and there was Jane Dowling, who I very much remembered. At six foot, she had been the tallest girl in our class. With here were Sheila Downs and her husband. Now that was another thing. When Jodie had said we'd be meeting Sheila and Jane there, I'd assumed she'd meant Sheila Jones, one of the class beauties, blonde and slim. So I was staggered to see this plump and definitely matronly person. I searched her face, discreetly I hoped, but could identify no recognizable feature. Mind you, she was very much more friendly, warm and jokey than snooty young Sheila had ever been, so I concluded that she had mellowed with age into a much nicer person. It was only when I got back into the car with Jodie to continue our journey that I realized my mistake. Sheila Downs had been the plumpest girl in our class and I can see her now struggling to climb up the ropes in the gym, with the teacher saying encouragingly, "Now come on, you you can do it if you try".

I remember feeling sorry for her as she clearly couldn't and never did manage to heave herself up and used to swing despairingly at the bottom of the rope going rather red.

But I'm getting side tracked. Where was I, or more to the point quo vadis? To Lesters for that reunion. Well, we got there and I walked apprehensively into the reception area. Everybody was already there. I suppose there were about thirty in all, including quite a lot of husbands. Two girls detached themselves from one of the little groups and bore down on me.

'Maria Ramos' they cried and hugged me in turn. I can't remember what I said, I felt so overwhelmed and I didn't know who the hell they were. Everybody looked so old to me, but what did I expect, we were all sixty eight by now and time and tide wait for no man. But I suppose like most of us, because you feel the same inside, you don't realize the passage of time affects us all. I suppose that they knew me, as I was the only stranger in the camp, for they had all, with the exception of me, kept in touch with regular meetings over the years. To be truthful, I only recognized two of them. Strangely enough, one of them was the afore mentioned Sheila Jones, who had hardly altered at all, apart from being an older version of her young self and looking as superior as ever, but actually being extremely nice to me. I remembered how I'd looked up to her from afar in the class. I was always so conscious of being from a poorer background than most of the other girls, whilst they were mostly very posh. She was one of the chosen ones, clever, pretty and good at everything. What's more, she had a name that I would have died for! How I'd longed to change my monica for an ordinary name like hers, or Mary Brown or Pam Davenport. Funnily enough Pam told me at the reunion that she'd envied my name. I was amazed!

"So exotic"! she said. If only she'd told me that at the time. Ah, Pam Davenport, the most beautiful girl in the school, let along our class. And she was here, still beautiful, but different somehow. Then one of the other girls told me that she had lost two daughters to cystic fibrosis at seven and fourteen. She still had her two sons thank goodness and that her faith had sustained her. And that was another thing, they were all practicing Catholics, for we had attended a Convent school, but unlike them, I had lapsed when I married. I had worried that that might create a barrier between them and me, but religion wasn't discussed, thank God! Oops, old habits die hard!

Probably thanks to their religious beliefs, most of them had been quite prolific and photos of their families were brandished proudly. Quiet and shy Veronica Timms had married her boss, a solicitor and had five children, all with excellent careers and had nine grandchildren so far. Davina Owen had five handsome sons who were all professionals, from doctors to accountants and innumerable grandchildren, with yet another on the way. Jane Dowling had three sons, two of whom stood in their lavishly be-medalled uniforms as soldiers currently serving in Iraq.

Barbara Britton had had nine miscarriages, yes nine, before finally having three children and had still found the time to successfully run their own pub. Susan Makepeace had emigrated to America with her husband when she was twenty two. She had then had twins when she was forty and returned to England with them as a destitute single mother when they were two years old. She'd used the word 'escaped' and as her husband had been Iranian, I sensed that hereby hung a tale, but was too polite to ask. Sheila Jones, Gemma Davis and Ann Treadwell all had four apiece and Sheila Downs had a mere three. My head was reeling. Thank goodness for Jodie, my chauffeur, who had never married and didn't have any. But it wasn't all good news, for she went on to say that she'd been a foster mum and that in fact one of them at thirty one still lived with her. Jodie had been a schoolteacher, as indeed had most of the girls, though they were all now retired. Quo vadis? Whither goest thou? I suppose the answer is down memory lane. Was it worth it? Yes, it had been a good experience and a memorable weekend, the weather had been lovely and so had the food and accommodation. It had been great meeting all my old classmates again, but some of the memories stirred up had been a little uncomfortable because I had always felt a little bit of an outsider, a bit of a fraud. Partly I suppose because I had been a convert, not the genuine dyed in the wool, born to it Catholic, like all of the others. And that was because I had left my Church of England school as I had been bullied as a small child and the only other nearby school was a catholic one, St Dominics. Surreal? You can bet your life it was,

but I was glad that I'd summoned up the courage to do something that I was really in the end quite afraid of facing up to.

WAGONS HO

J G Dyer

Friday night again and the four of us are standing at the corner, with our one shilling pocket money burning a hole in our pocket, wondering what picture to see, Teddy and Geordie love westerns as I do, Woodrow likes gangsters and hoodlums, but he is out voted, so it is the Plaza, a newly built cinema showing Wagon Train West, starring Hoot Gibson, Buck Jones, Tom Mix and Gloria Swanson. With such a cast it was really settled and off we went. Reaching the picture house, we queued outside for the second show. Suddenly as expected, we were spotted by the manager. "I want no trouble from you lot, no standing and no shouting ok". We agreed not to do anything wrong. You see it is always daft Geordie,Teddy's brother, he gets carried away and tonight his favourite (and mine) Hoot Gibson was the star. We all warned Buck (Geordie's nickname) and he promised faithfully to be quiet, he promised to 'simmer doon and keep cool'. We all knew that Buck couldn't keep cool in a tub of ice cream.
At last the first show came out with some of the kids shooting at each other as they rode their bucking 'bronco's home to their ranch, then we were allowed to enter and get our tickets, three pence each. As we reached the door, the manager was tearing the tickets in half. "Mind what I said now you lot, behave or you are out". There were four seats together, front row second block and there we sat waiting, listening to records of Riding the Range, Lonesome Cowboy and Tumbling Tumble Weeds, sung of course by the Barber Shop Choir, Gene Autry or Roy Rogers and the Western Aires. We sat through the adverts, the Gaumont news, a couple of cartoons of Bugs Bunny (my favourite) then the music strikes up for the picture, the small curtain slides open 'MGM proudly presents Wagon Train West'. Geordie leans across "Hey man, Hoots in it, he'll wipe the floor with them" he yells. I knew it "Quiet" I hiss.
"He will get us thrown out again" says Woody. The picture starts and whenever Hoot Gibson or Buck Jones are killing the Indians,

Teddy and Buck are on their feet "Go on Hoot, give it to them, watch out Buck, Red Clouds behind you, chop his head off Tom". This went on all through the film, why we were not thrown out I will never know. Maybe it was because some of the others were carried away by it all and the manager could not throw everybody out.

On the way down, we called for one pint before going home. Woodrow and Geordie kept arguing on and on. "Did you see Hoot kill Red Cloud, he shot him on the move" said Geordie. "So did Tom Mix" said Woodrow. "How" yelled Teddy "he was dead, Hoot shot him, I saw him fall". We were now in the local having our one and only pint. Woodrow had to start again "I will tell you how Tom Mix shot him, those Indians have to be killed three times before they get paid, Indian Chief's twice". Geordie was having nothing of this. "We all saw him, Hoot killed four Indians and Red Cloud, we saw them fall off their horses". Woodrow took a sip of his pint and without looking at Teddy or Buck "Then they got back on their horses again, so that Tom Mix could shoot them off again". "You're a liar" screamed Geordie, he was really upset now. "Hoot shot them dead, I saw them fall off them nags dead". I tried to calm things down. "Let's drop it, we are causing a scene. It was of no use.

Buck started again "our cowboys have killed more than your rotten gangsters". Teddy joined in "I'll say they have, in one picture they killed all of them outright". "If you say so, but I know different, gangsters don't kill Indians" replied Woodrow. "No" cried Buck "cause they are cowards and they can't ride horses". We had almost finished our pint when the manager said we would have to leave because of the argument. All the way home, the bickering went on. According to Geordie and brother Teddy, Hoot Gibson, Tom Mix and Buck Jones had killed the whole Cheyenne nation, the Sioux and Blackfoot nations, plus ninety per cent of the Navahos and Mohicans, while Woodrow's gangsters had killed one puny pick pocket who had held the pistol to his own head in case they missed.

"All right, all right" yelled Woodrow "instead of going for a pint tomorrow night, let us go to the Plaza again, we will count the

Indians and see who shoots them if you dare". "You're on" was the reply. "Our cowboys are the greatest, will you come Joe?" "Yes" I sighed "I'll come, if it is only to keep the peace". They were still bickering as we wished each goodnight and departed. Saturday night we met again at the corner, we spent an hour deciding who was to count how many Indians had been shot, who shot them and how many remounted their horses to be shot again.

Plus, to top it all, who killed Red Cloud and how many times. Geordie I suppose had been working all night, as he gave us all a piece of paper and a pencil. "I want this done right" he said "no cheating, right and proper, no favourites".

He had us swear on the bible, even his brother Teddy. When all this had been done, we made our way to the Plaza, the first show was over and the second show was just starting to go in, so there was no waiting. We bought our tickets and as the manager halved them, he looked at us in surprise "You again" he said, "No noise or you are out, alright?" We got our seats and waited as the news, cartoons and adverts were being shown. Buck, Teddy and Woodrow were shaking their fists at each other with "Now we will see who kills who, now we will find out who is the greatest. Looking daggers at each other. The curtains closed, at last I thought, thank heavens. "Now" yelled Buck, eyeball to eyeball with Woodrow "now is the moment, get your pencils out".

The curtains reopened again and there it was, the Lions roar and 'MGM proudly presents FLASH GORDON in "THE VENUS FLY CATCHER".

No one had noticed the bill boards changed on Friday night. They can't get any satisfaction.

THE IMPERFECT STORM

Vera Downes

The sun was setting over the valley when I first saw the cottage and it was love at first sight.

The property was in the Cotswolds and had originally been built as a primitive Methodist Chapel approximately 200 years ago, but had now been roughly converted to private living accommodation. We hoped to make improvements and eventually retire there.

The improvements proved to be massive, starting with a new roof.....but that's another story.

During the forthcoming upheaval, my husband had to go away on business, which was unfortunate as I had always had a mortal fear of the dark, but decided to stay there alone except for my two cats and overcome my fears by power of will.

The night was dark and the clouds scudding across the moon foretold the approach of a coming storm. The wind rose higher and began to moan. The tarpaulin sheeting on the roof, in the absence of tiles, began to flap wildly as the lightening flashed and the thunder grew ever louder.

There was no electricity, drains or floor. The access to my bedroom was by a ladder and a plank and my only light was a calor gas lamp loaned by a friend.

My two companions, siamese cats, were under the bed clothes, fur standing on end and eyes illuminated in the violent flashes of blue lightning, the rain was deafening. The wind reached a new pitch of ferocity and through the gaps in the roofing I could see the ridge of the escarpment etched by the elements. At the height of the conflagration, the lamp failed and my isolation was complete, for to locate the ladder or the plank was impossible.

After what seemed an eternity, the clamour of the storm abated and an eerie silence pervaded over the whole of the golden valley.

After a while the cats reared out of their coverings, having been alerted by something..... Yes, there was definitely the furtive sound of footsteps which finally stopped at our door.

I had expected us to be discovered stiff and cold by the cold light of day - however, we survived - just. When the dawn broke and chased away the clouds of night, we discovered signs of foraging when we descended the ladder and all our food stocks were missing.

No doubt our visitor had been a badger, fox or maybe the 'Black Beast Of Bodmin' - we shall never know.

THE CHARITY SHOP

Beryl Risbridger

As she put the key in the door, Betty Metcalf felt a thrill of anticipation. Ever since she had been managing the Oxfam Shop, this was the first time they had been given a whole house to deal with. Usually it was a few bits and pieces of furniture or clothing, but this was the biggest legacy they had been left.

The deceased had a been a single lady, apparently very reserved and her only living relatives lived in Canada and had left all the dealings to a local Solicitor who was the Executor of the Will. He had given carte blanche to Betty, provided the whole house was cleared. Betty had rallied all the helpers she could and had managed to persuade a local removal company to load all the furniture and even to store the larger pieces for free, provided they got the maximum publicity. She had been to the house and taken an Inventory of the contents; decided what items should be delivered direct to the shop and the rest to go to the removers depository. All the clothes had been put into boxes and would need to be sorted out, priced and put on display. Even a cursory look had Betty feeling quite excited and somewhat surprised. She had only known the lady very slightly and had thought of her as a 'Miss Marple' type, wearing sensible clothes and shoes, but what she had seen already in the wardrobe made this debatable.

Unable to settle, Betty found herself walking to the door and glancing out to see if the van was arriving. "Do hurry up" she thought impatiently.

At last the van turned the corner and drew up outside the shop. Everything had to be unloaded as speedily as possible because of the parking restrictions and within a short period of time, everything that was being delivered to the shop was off the van, which then sped away with the remainder of the furniture.

Although it was quite a large piece, Betty had wanted the bureau to come to the shop as it was full of papers, boxes of letters and photos and she couldn't wait to go through it, although she felt she couldn't do this when customers were in the shop and had decided that she would do it in her own time.

Leaving her volunteers to run the shop, Betty decided to start sorting out the clothes from the boxes in the room behind the shop.

In a plastic cover was a beautiful real fur coat. Betty was not sure what the skin was, but she ran her hand over it and marvelled at its lovely softness. If it turned out to be mink, it would be worth a lot of money, even if nowadays real fur was unpopular. She could not resist trying it on and immediately felt a lot richer somehow. Standing in front of the full length mirror, she could hardly believe how different she seemed to look.

Obviously there were quite a few sensible clothes, such as tweed skirts, twin sets, long sleeved blouses and flat, laced up shoes, as one would expect, but Betty could hardly believe the lovely, pure silk underwear she found neatly folded in pillow cases. There were several luggage cases and Betty eagerly tried to undo them, only to be disappointed to find them locked, but where were the keys? The only place Betty could think of looking for them was in the bureau, although that would probably be like looking for a needle in a haystack! Much as she wanted to start searching straightaway, there was a shop to run and she reluctantly abandoned the task for the time being.

Any other day Betty would have been pleased that the shop was so busy, but today would have been glad of a quieter day. During a lull, her other assistants were anxious to hear what they had got to deal with and Betty told them about the fur coat and the underwear.

"You did say that all this stuff came from Miss Parker's house, didn't you Betty?" asked Joan Brown, looking very puzzled. Joan had lived locally all her life and was the type that generally knew everything about everyone, but she could hardly believe that Miss Parker could possibly have owned this sort of thing. She thought that Miss Parker had arrived in the town about 20 years ago and moved into a cottage close to the town centre. She had become a regular member of the Church and had been thought to be a pleasant person, but never seemed to make any really close friends. Over the years it had somehow become accepted that Miss Parker was a retired Librarian, although where this had come from wasn't clear, but possibly because she seemed to have a great love of books and was frequently seen in the book shop in the High Street.

"I just can't imagine a dear old lady like Miss Parker ever having any other sort of life where she would wear this type of thing" wondered Joan, her fertile imagination already going into overdrive!

As for Betty, she could hardly contain herself to find out more about this puzzle.

Having spent a restless night, she went to the shop two hours earlier than usual, determined to search for the missing keys, which she hoped might be in the bureau. She began to systematically sift through the two drawers, but with no success.

In the quest for the keys, needless to say, other intriguing things had come to light and Betty felt even more excited to find out about the late Miss Parker and her past.

There was a rapping on the window and Betty realised that the hours had flown by and it was time to open the shop. Unable to resist it, Betty took out a box from the drawer which she then hastily closed, before opening the door to Joan Brown; she really didn't want Joan poking around and perhaps gossiping about it before she had been able to form her own opinion. Knowing the opportunity was unlikely to occur during the day, Betty slipped the box into her bag and could hardly contain herself until closing time finally arrived and she was on her way home. Usually she was ready for her evening meal, but not tonight.

Making a quick cup of tea, she took this into her neat front room, together with the box, settled herself on her comfy sofa and opened it up. On the top were photographs, mostly of views and buildings, just the odd one had people in it. Underneath there were several packs of envelopes, tied together with ribbon, presumably with letters in them. Fighting with her conscience, she reluctantly put them aside and although she was dying to undo the ribbon and see what the envelopes contained, she felt they might be very personal and to read them could be an intrusion into Miss Parker's privacy. "How would you feel girl, if someone was reading your letters" she chided herself, but couldn't resist noticing that the top letter was indeed addressed to Patricia Parker, the address was in London and the date stamp was 1944. Betty's fingers itched, but she resisted the temptation, at least for that moment. Beneath the letters were a number of theatre programmes and her first thought was how small they were against those of today and only cost a shilling or two. Sifting through them, she noticed that most of them were musicals and one or two by Ivor Novello. A wave of nostalgia overwhelmed her as she remembered her own Mother had spoken to her often about how wonderful Novello's music had been during the War when she had been in London whilst on leave from the WAAF's and she and her boyfriend, who eventually became her Father, held hands and lost themselves in romantic shows such as 'Perchance to Dream' and 'Kings Rhapsody'.

Snapping herself back, somewhat reluctantly to the present day, she began looking more closely at the photographs. She had not previously realised that there was faded, but still readable writing on the back of each of them. There was one of Wellington Harbour in New Zealand dated June 1937. Another was of Tokyo in Japan, dated August 1937. There was another from San Francisco taken October 1937 and so they went on round the world up till July 1939. Had Miss Parker taken all of them herself or had they been sent to her from someone else, Betty wondered, none the wiser so far of what Miss Parker's life had been.

Bedtime came all too soon, but Betty spent a restless night and try as she might, she could not put Miss Parker and her mysterious life out of her mind. She must have dropped off eventually, but felt completely exhausted when her alarm clock woke her up. Feeling better after a quick shower, a couple cups of coffee and a slice of toast, Betty was ready to face the world again. No chance of getting to the shop early this morning, she thought regretfully.

It was much quieter today and between herself, Joan and another helper, they began to sort out Miss Parker's clothes. It was quite simple to price the clothes that Miss Parker had worn in the village, but the silk underwear and especially the fur coat, were an unknown quantity. Betty couldn't resist trying the coat on again whilst the other two were at lunch and she really hated the thought of selling it to someone else. She decided she would ask their Area Manager to price it when he next came, although she didn't know if she could afford it, nor when she would wear it, even if she were able to buy it, but she did feel so good in it.

Closing time finally arrived and Betty slipped another box into her bag to take home. This one seemed to contain diaries and she thought that these might shed more light on Miss Parker's past.

After a hasty meal, Betty began to read. The first entry was May 1937 and said "left Southampton this morning. The ship is so luxurious; cannot believe that I am actually here. My cabin is quite small, but well fitted. There is another bed and I wonder if I will have to share?" The last sentence puzzled Betty. "Surely she must have known when she booked that she might be sharing; surely that would have affected the cost?"

Reading on, it became obvious that Miss Parker was not a passenger, but a member of the crew, although it was not clear what she actually did. The diary was full of avid descriptions of where the ship stopped and her excitement and her anticipation at actually seeing these places came through in her entries.

Betty found herself becoming more and more involved with trying to solve the mystery of Miss Parker. It was almost becoming an obsession. She was convinced that the missing keys would provide the answer to the enigma, but where could they be?

Her Area Manager called in and was amazed of the quality of everything amongst Miss Parker's possessions. He confessed that he had no idea what price the fur coat should be offered at and he would have to do some research about this.

Over the next few weeks, the goods were priced and put on display. They were snapped up almost immediately, making a great deal of money for the charity. The staff were meticulous in keeping a note of every transaction, so that the Executor was satisfied everything was above board. This task fell to Betty and she became quite friendly with him. She told him about the luggage cases and how she had never managed to find the keys. He too, felt curious about Miss Parker's past, as he had only known her since she had arrived in the village some 20 years ago.

A couple of days later, the Solicitor, whose name was Brian Cooper, called into the shop. "After you left, I thought about all the keys we have collected over the years from various clients, so I've brought them just in case, however unlikely, one happens to fit the locks".

Without much confidence, Betty began to try every likely key into the locks, with no success. Despondently she put in yet another key and was amazed to hear a click! Unbelievably it opened a case and Betty gasped when rows of beautiful evening dresses were revealed. The mystery, far from being cleared up, had deepened!!

She phoned Brian and he came over in his lunch break. He was equally amazed at the contents and they were determined to solve the matter. Looking at the facts they did know, such as that the postcards stopped abruptly in July 1939, so what happened then? Well the obvious answer was that we were on the brink of the War. Yet the selection of programmes continued.

"I know you have reservations about reading the letters, Betty, but I can't see that there is any alternative. We seem to have exhausted everything else". "I suppose you are right, but you make the first move" and she handed the package over to him.

The last letter was dated 1944, so that was the first one they read. It was from a man which, reading between the lines, was one of the crew

160

on a bomber and was just off on a probably dangerous mission. He wrote of his feelings for her, but as this was the last letter, they assumed that sadly he hadn't returned.

Some of the other letters were from this man, but others were not. Some were saying how much they had enjoyed the show. What show, they wondered?

"Listen, we've decided she wasn't a passenger, but that she worked on the ships. So where would she be likely to wear these gorgeous evening dresses?" "Well, I reckon she was in the shows on the big liners".

"That's brilliant Brian, but how do we find out anything more?" "Let's have a look at those programmes and the other letters.

Inside one of them has a press notice form a magazine, praising Miss Patricia Parker's debut in a show in London after being discovered on a P&O Liner".

"Just like Jane MacDonald" Betty said. "If I hadn't been so reluctant at reading the letters before, we'd have found that out ages ago!!"

So the mystery was solved, but on one could believe that mousey Miss Parker was, at one time, a famous showgirl

Postscript
Did Betty, in the end, get the fur coat? Well, that's another story.

JIM BOY

John Rogers

We wus goen down the Mississippi to nu Orleans, cos Huck had stuck Mrs Farrington old sow to make her bleed all over the place, cos he didn't want any more of that there schooling he spread the blood every which way so that his Aunt would tink him a gonner, den he threw the old pig in the River Den. He axed me if I would help him run away, cos den I wouldn't be a slave no more. My name is Jim, I is very black, I been a slave for 19 years an I heard dat iffen I get to Norleans, I could be free. Thas why Ise helping Huck. He is a nice white boy an he treats me well. Dis old raft we're on is only empty cans and planks held together with bits of string and wire.

It is a lot of fun adrifting along liae dis. But wery dangerous in de day. The Revenue can't see me in tie dark cos I is so black and sometimes Huck has to hide in the water under the raft in de day.

We got plenty to eat, cost Huck raided his Aunt's store cupboard for sour belly pork and lots and lots of dem lovely sweet beans. We passed two neihts peacefully. I was nearly caught by a danged Snapping Turtle, the darned ting took I bit out of my finges. It is lovely floating down de river, but very dangerous, specially at night.

On our third night we had real trouble. A gang of dem other run away slaves crept on to our raft and dun stole all our vittles. Huck was very cross and cussed quite a bit, but I dun told him that "We could get plenty vittles in the fields as we went along. That cheered him up.

Another danger was dem great big paddle steamers up and down the river, with the Leadrmen a hollering "By the Mark Twain". We oft got a bit of a tow unknown to them. Sometimes Huck would creep aboard to steal some food, my little friend is very brave.

162

THE DELIVERY

Maureen O'Sullivan

It would be St Valentine's Day soon - the first since they had become engaged. Tracey wanted to give Giles something really special. Something different. She would show everyone just how much he meant to her.

She knew there had been talk when they first met and then became engaged. She could see it in the faces of his family and his colleagues at the stockbroking firm where he was a junior partner. Especially when she met their wives and girlfriends. Not classy enough, they thought. They were polite, of course, but she saw the way they looked her up and down when they thought she wasn't looking, taking in everything from her hairstyle to her shoes. No matter how much she spent on herself, the looks continued. She'd show them!

Tracey spent the whole of the Saturday afternoon before St Valentine's Day wandering around Bluewater, looking for the perfect gift. She wouldn't be flashy and buy something expensive, which they would expect her to do. No, it would be something of special value, something unique and meaningful. She ended up buying it the day before Valentine's Day. She gift wrapped it herself. This was one thing she was very good at. The gift box looked beautiful with its silver and navy paper and ribbons. She put the smaller box into a larger, plain one, wrapped it in brown paper and sealed in carefully with parcel tape. She addressed it in large clear letters to Giles at his office. She'd arranged to have it hand delivered by courier. She couldn't risk it being delayed in the post.

The following morning Giles found his card on the kitchen worktop by the coffee jar. Tracey was still in bed. He started work at 7 so was always up and out before she'd stirred. Opening the card he read the message inside. "Love you up to the sky" she'd written. "You will get your present later". He smiled to himself, wondering what she had planned. He'd sent her roses, a huge bouquet - they would be delivered later.

163

Later that morning as he sat at his computer desk in the open plan offices, a parcel was placed in front of him by one of the post room staff. He was on the telephone to Hong Kong, settling a multi million pound deal, so it was some time before he could concentrate on the parcel. Unwrapping it, he withdrew the extravagantly wrapped gift box. It was too late to be discrete.

"What have we here", called Justin Farquharson in a deliberately loud voice. "A Valentine's gift from the divine Tracey from Tottenham" he boomed, to raucous laughter.

His colleagues gathered around Giles desk, anxious to see the contents of the gift box.

Off came the silver and navy paper. Off came the lid of the box. Off came layer upon layer of snowy white tissue paper. Giles pulled out a white plastic box. He was smiling as he popped off the lid. Everyone leaned closer. Nestling in a bed of silver foil was a blood red heart! A real heart! Giles stopped smiling. No one laughed. They all turned away, one or two of them retching into their handkerchiefs, others, shaking their heads in pitiful disbelief.

Giles grabbed the box and ran out of the office, down the corridor and into the Gents toilets. Only thinking that he wanted to be rid of the thing, he threw the heart into the toilet bowl and flushed it. As the flushing stopped, to his dismay he saw that the heart had popped back to the surface and was sitting there bobbing on the top of the water. He flushed it again and again before it finally disappeared.

Giles did not realise then that later that day the heart would bob up again just us his unknowing elderly senior partner pulled up his pin striped trousers and flushed the toilet. He then, almost in a state of collapse, rushed to his office and telephoned his GP saying that there was something terribly wrong with him, that he needed a very urgent appointment.

WAITING AT NAN'S PANTRY

Marion Osborn

If only I'd realized what the job entailed I wouldn't have applied, but I didn't, so I did. "Have you any bar staff vacancies" I'd asked politely.

In retrospect, the man on the other end of the phone had seemed over enthusiastic, particularly when I'd said I was experienced. "No need for an interview" he'd said to my surprise, "just turn up at eight this evening. How much do we pay? Oh, it's twenty pounds a session". This had seemed a king's ransom to me. "Oh and we do like our staff to wear white blouses and a black skirt. We are late tonight. Oh you knew that? We finish at two o'clock. Do you have a car? No? Never mind we pay for a cab home. Marion you said? Look forward to seeing you later".

So duly attired as requested, I'd turned up. The place was called 'Nan's Pantry Banqueting Suite' and that should have given me a clue, but it didn't. Talk about naive! It looked much bigger close up I thought. I knew it by sight, but had only passed it on the bus as I went to Ilford. I went inside and was directed to join a little group of people waiting in the foyer. Then a man, who I presumed to be the manager, came over to us. After he'd been speaking for a few minutes it dawned on me that he was expecting us all to wait on tables at various functions, from Barmitzvahs to Weddings. These were going on in different rooms all over the building. I was horrified, but too nervous to tell him I'd never done what amounted to silver service waiting. Most of the group had obviously worked there before and he simply told them which rooms to go to. And then he was left with another girl, who looked a bit snooty, and me, and my heart sank.

"Follow me" he ordered and after him we went, through various rooms thronging with people, then up an iron staircase, then down a long, long corridor and then down a small staircase, until we came to a kitchen. I thought I'd died and gone to hell! It was like a madhouse, flustered people rushing about shouting and swearing. The heat and the smells were over powering. I remember noticing a frowsy looking woman washing up mounds of dishes in a large butler sink and as she looked round at us, she said to the man "The dish washer has conked again". He simply shrugged and mumbled "Keep up the good work Brenda. I'll get it looked at"

I remember thinking, "Poor worn out thing, she must have been pretty once". But my thoughts soon came back to my own situation. I knew I had to come clean when I was handed a metal contraption, which became heavier and heavier as one of the kitchen staff started to load plates of steaming soup on to it. I looked round desperately and if I could have found my way out of this maze like building I would have run for it, but pathfinder I am not.

"I've never done this before. I thought it was just a bar job" I stammered. The manager looked at me coldly, "You'll just have to do your best. Wendy will show you the ropes" and with that he was gone.

I didn't hold out much hope from the snooty one, so I mentally switched off and went into automatic pilot. And thus began one of the most ghastly evenings I have ever spent.

"Serve to the right" was the sum of Wendy's instructions, or was it to the left? I'll never know. With trepidation I walked into the huge banqueting room with my soups. I might have looked the part in my smart black and white outfit, but I hadn't a clue of what I was doing. The room was full of big tables around which there seemed to me to be hundreds of people expectantly waiting to be fed. Talk about Nightmare City! Then it was just toing and froing from the kitchen to get more and more food and because I wasn't sure whether I'd got it all wrong, I kept apologizing every time I served anyone. It was finally over and everyone had been served and eaten their fill and I breathed a sigh of relief. But not for long, as we now had to take orders for after dinner liquers.

"This will be where your bar experience will come in handy" said Wendy who was really quite nice when we had a chance to speak. "You take orders round the table and then get the drinks from the bar and when you bring them back collect the money. A good tip is to clock the first person and work round the table from there so that you know who ordered what".

I was so grateful for her advice, but when I came back with the tray of drinks, I couldn't help exclaiming "Oh no". To my horror a lot of them had changed places and completely mucked up my sequence. One of the men at the table noticed my horror stricken face. To my eternal gratitude, although he laughed, he took pity on me and not only distributed the drinks to the right people, but also collected the money for me. He even engineered a tip for me and slipped a fiver into my blouse pocket.

In my innocence I thought that was the end of my ordeal, but no, it was to be a long night. We were directed from that room to another, where there was another function and the process was all repeated. In some rooms speeches were being made. I remember having to walk across the centre of one with a tray of drinks, self consciously praying I wouldn't trip up in my high heels and drop the lot while everyone was looking at me. And so it went on, being rushed from room to room, endlessly serving and clearing up, throughout the night until two o'clock at last arrived.

We then all gathered in the foyer to collect our wages and await our cabs. I was given my money first and when the manager asked me if I'd be coming back, my "No thank you!" was so fervent that everybody, including him, laughed uproariously.

TOWNSEND

John Rogers

There was a pre-fab Village called Townsend by the side of the Hainault Estate where all the people were friendly and regard for each other was great. There was a communal hut built for them, for pure recreation and fun. Which bound them closer, each and everyone.

There was a group called the Townsend Players doing plays and sketches and such, directed by Mrs Fubini who had a true actor's touch.

A certain air pervaded that place, so calm safe and secure, even the few shops were courteous and friendly with a charm that beggared belief. It seemed that each one of the community felt safe there with a notable sense of relief, no sign now remains of those war years, wiped clean, now just grass.

Overall, only one shop remains 'Bennetts' Newsagents, Manford Way, where one may still experience the same old world gracious treatment of years gone by.

MEET THE AUTHORS

Ivy Brown

Creative Writing is my latest hobby. My first was Amateur Dramatics. I joined a group when I was in my late teens and for eight years acted in many plays, including 'This Happy Breed, The Barrett's of Wimpole Street and Rebecca'.
I would probably have carried on for much longer, but the stage we used was removed and the hall became a ballroom.
So I started going to art classes and have been painting ever since. I prefer landscapes and like to paint outdoors, but only when the weather is fine.

Jim Burns

As founder member of the 'Hainault Creative Writers' I am amazed that a chance encounter with Alan Hemmings put the wheels rolling to our newly formed Writers Group in the Working Man's Club. I showed Alan the map of the London Underground and asked if he could make a book cover. So our first book 'Hainault, The End of the Line' was born. Now after six books published and a new one called 'Carousel' on its way, we are now embedded in the Hainault Forest Community Centre. My personal and proudest memory was the writers involvement in a play called 'Gas Mask on My Shoulder' in co-operation with Hainault High School. The story of war time evacuation, the youths playing our roles. It was a great success. Playing in local centres, Town Hall, Barbican Centre, Hyde Park, to commemorate the 1939-1945 war. May we go from strength to strength.
Extract from the Barbican Performance Leaflet
'LONDON BOROUGH OF REDBRIDGE. Gasmask on my Shoulder was devised from the wartime experiences of the Hainault Community Association Writers Group in collaboration with Spare Tyre Theatre Company, students of Hainault Forest High School and dancers from the Hainault Youth Dance Group'.

Joseph G Dyer

I was born in Blaydon, three miles from Newcastle. After the three 'R's, an offered place at the local Technical College was declined through lack of funds, leaving school before the age of fourteen to become a miner.

I later worked as a metal pourer and furnace man at a local foundry. Around 1952 I came to London working at Ford Motors, then for many years at Barking Brassware until finally retiring from Lesney Matchbox Toys at the age of 72. I joined the Hainault Writers Group two years ago, pleased to have participated in the making of this book.

Michael Fabb

I have been writing for a number of years, mostly in a business environment and now since my retirement on health grounds, am now writing short stories on a regular basis for the Hainault Writers Group.

I also write on an occasional basis, short stories and articles for a local church magazine, which is widely read throughout South East Essex. Apart from my short stories, there are three novels simmering on the back burner awaiting completion.

Marion Osborn

I was educated at St Angela's Ursuline Convent in Forest Gate. I worked in a wide variety of occupations. When I retired I joined the Hainault Community Centre Writers' Group.

Maureen O'Sullivan

I was born in East London during the war. My mother was an Irishwoman, father a Londoner who, after the war, went into teaching, his lifelong passion. We moved to Essex and I was educated at the Ilford Ursuline Convent. I worked in the City for half my working life, the other half for the Local Education Authority. I retired two years ago.

I am married with two children, three grandchildren and one on the way. My interests, besides writing, are reading, the theatre, church work and my family and friends.

I am one of the newer members of the Writing Group, joining eighteen months ago. Having written on and off for most of my life, it is only now with the support and encouragement of my fellow writers that I have begun to write regularly.

This little book will give some you idea of our work - diverse, as we are - but we hope you enjoy it.

Beryl Risbridger

I've belonged to Hainault Creative Writers Group for 19 years and it has helped me so much, having been widowed 20 years ago and wondering what to do with my future.

There have been many changes in Members, but we've always become good friends. We've had many laughs, also tears and learned a great deal about others lives.

As an only child with loving Parents, I've not experienced some of the traumas others have had.

One of my biggest regrets is that the War disrupted my Education so badly.

However, I've been blessed with a good, generally happy life.

John Rogers

Me Rog. Her. Mrs

Born 1923 in Ireland

Kidnapped 1933 to England
Very basic education
Worked hard for the Nation
In the process having fun
Jack the lad of all trades
Master of course of none
Joined the Hainault Writers
In the dim and distant past
Learnt to spell my name, at last
Please forgive my brevity
This is no time for levity
No prevarication, no lies
Who am I? Surprise, surprise

B-a-r-t-h--o-l-o-m-e-w J-o-h-n R-o-g-e-r-s
See!

Arthur Salton

Born in Bow, East London in 1928. Times were hard, becoming worse, when war started in 1939 living through the air raids on London. As the war ended I went into the Navy and was in it for six and half years. Out in 1952, I married and we had two children. We moved to Hainault in 1957 and it was in 1995 when I discovered Hainault Writers, got hooked on writing and the writers and and have been with them ever since and hope to keep on writing till the end of the road.

Vera Downes

I am grateful to have experienced a varied and interesting life and a busy one, as I had jobs for most of the time in order to pay for my other activities.

When I was born my brother was 22 and a half years my senior and already in business. He was my idol and instilled in me a desire to see the world, which I have mostly done, from seeing the sun rise over the Himalayas on the Tibetan highway to tiger tracking on the back of an elephant in S. India and Cambodia and many experiences in the Masai Mara.

I lived between Essex and the Cotswolds from 1969 - 2003, meeting many 'interesting people' including Jilly Cooper who lived in the nearby village and used the local hostelry with her husband, Leo.

I am passionately fond of animals, both wild and domesticated and am interested in gardening and decorating.

I met my husband in 1949 and we agreed to marry after 24 hours. It was a very happy liaison which only ended recently with his death, so the joint ventures are now all in the past.

Hazel Dongworth (b.1947, Woodford, Essex) a retired teacher with a 34 year old son, lives in Woodford. Taught English for 35 years in East London and Essex until 2007. Started writing poems in 1980 a few years after her divorce. Member of Stratford Poets, an East London Poetry group for many years. A year after the loss of her partner, joined the Hainault Writers Group.

Margot S Cooper. My mother influenced my learning and my Sisters would read to me. I went to Romford Technical School and then to college. I worked as a part time teacher, Chef Lecturer at Westminster College, but now retired. I paint, do flower arranging, am a Member of the Woodford Flower Club and a member on the Editorial Board of Flower Arranging Magazine.